Towers

William K. Durr
Jean M. LePere
John J. Pikulski

Consultant:
Hugh Schoephoerster

HOUGHTON MIFFLIN COMPANY   **BOSTON**

Atlanta   Dallas   Geneva, Illinois   Hopewell, New Jersey   Palo Alto   Toronto

Acknowledgments

Grateful acknowledgment is given for the contributions of Paul McKee.

For each of the selections listed below, grateful acknowledgment is made for permission to adapt and/or reprint copyrighted material, as follows:

"Birthdays," adapted text of "Birthdays," from *Little Owl, Keeper of the Trees*, by Ronald and Ann Himler. Test copyright © 1974 by Ronald and Ann Himler. Used by permission of Harper & Row, Publishers, Inc.

"The Brave Baby Sitter," adapted from *The Bravest Babysitter*, by Barbara Greenberg. Copyright © 1977 by Barbara Greenberg. Reprinted by permission of The Dial Press.

"Busy Carpenters," by James S. Tippett. From the book *Busy Carpenters* by James S. Tippett, published by World in 1929. Reprinted by permission of Martha K. Tippett.

"Butterfly, butterfly," from *Music of Acoma, Isleta, Cochiti and Zuni Pueblos* by Frances Densmore: Butterfly song, page 38. From *Smithsonian Institution Bureau of American Ethnology*, Bulletin 165. Washington, D.C.: Government Printing Office, 1957. Reprinted by permission of the Smithsonian Institution Press.

"Child of the Navajos," from *Child of the Navajos*, by Seymour Reit. Copyright © 1971 by Seymour Reit. Reprinted by permission of Dodd, Mead & Company, Inc.

"City," by Langston Hughes, from *The Langston Hughes Reader*. Copyright ©1958 by Langston Hughes. Reprinted by permission of Harold Ober Associates Incorporated.

"Fidelia," adapted from *Fidelia*, by Ruth Adams. Text copyright © 1970 by Ruth Adams. Used by permission of Lothrop, Lee & Shepard Inc. (a division of William Morrow & Co.)

"Following Directions," adapted from *Paper Capers: All Kinds of Things to Make With Paper*, by Florence Temko. Copyright © 1974 by Florence Temko. Used by permission of Four Winds Press, a Division of Scholastic Magazines, Inc.

"The Giant," from *All That Sunlight*, by Charlotte Zolotow. Text copyright © 1967 by Charlotte Zolotow. Reprinted by permission of Harper & Row, Publishers, Inc.

"Gladys Told Me to Meet Her Here," adapted from *Gladys Told Me to Meet Her Here*, by Marjorie Weinman Sharmat. Text copyright © 1970 by Marjorie Weinman Sharmat. Used by permission of Harper & Row, Publishers, Inc.

"Go Wind," from *I Feel the Same Way*, by Lilian Moore. Copyright © 1967 by Lilian Moore. Reprinted by permission of Atheneum Publishers.

(Acknowledgments and Artist Credits are continued on page 304.)

Printed in the U.S.A.

ISBN: 0-395-31940-4

Contents

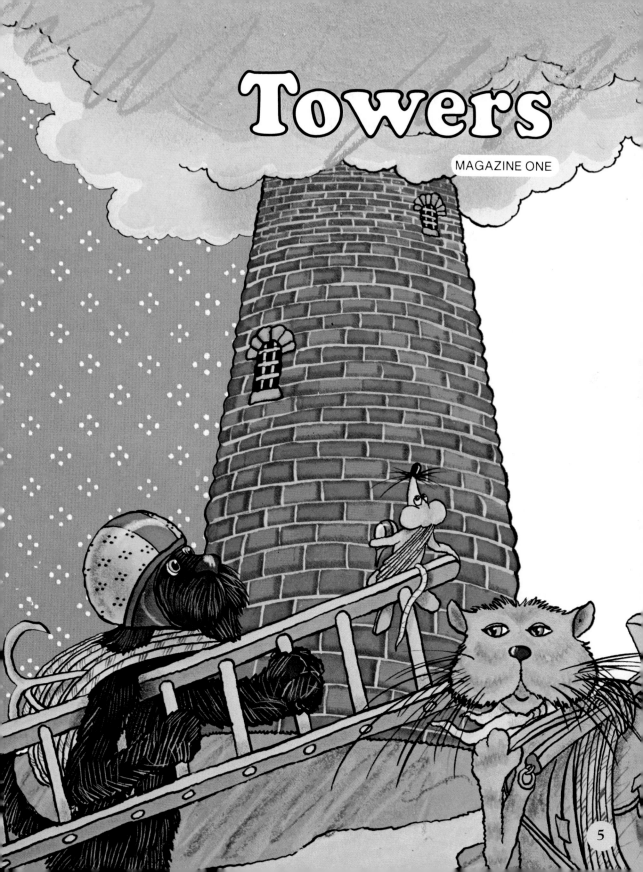

Towers

MAGAZINE ONE

Contents

Birthdays

by RONALD and ANN HIMLER

Little Owl turned over in his bed.
He listened to the rain falling on the leaves
outside. He liked the sound of rain.
He liked it so much he fell asleep.

When he woke up, the rain had stopped.
All at once, Little Owl sat up.

"Tonight is my birthday!" he cried.
He jumped out of bed and ran into the kitchen.

"Good evening, Little Owl," Mother said
with a smile. "Are you ready for breakfast?"

"Yes, I'm hungry," said Little Owl. He sat
down at the table. "Do you know what
tonight is?"

"Yes, I do," said Mrs. Owl. And she gave
Little Owl two big pieces of bread and butter.
"Tonight is the night I must clean the windows."

"No, no!" said Little Owl. "I mean, do you
know what *tonight* is? It's a special night."

Mother laughed. "Special? There's nothing
special about cleaning windows."

After breakfast, Little Owl went outside.
"She forgot," he said to himself. He went
down the steps of the Old Tree. "She forgot
that tonight is my birthday. This never
happened before."

Little Owl walked slowly to the tall trees.
He saw Raccoon sitting under a tree. "Hi,
Raccoon," said Little Owl. "Do you know
what tonight is?"

"Sure I do," said Raccoon.

"You do?" cried Little Owl.

"Tonight is the night Bear promised to show me her secret fishing place," said Raccoon.

"Oh," said Little Owl. "I thought you *knew*."

"I've been waiting here a long time," Raccoon went on. "But Bear hasn't come yet. And I can't wait any longer. I'm going down to the old rock by the river and fish."

"Can I come?" asked Little Owl.

"Listen, Little Owl," said Raccoon. "You know what you can do? When Bear comes by, tell her I'm down at the river. Will you do that, Little Owl?"

Then Raccoon ran off without waiting for an answer.

11

Little Owl was left alone. He stood
for a while, looking down the path.
But no one came.

"I'm not going to stand here all night,"
he thought. "Not on my birthday."

Little Owl wrote a note for Bear and stuck it
on the tree. Then he stepped back and looked
at the note.

"What if that note were a sign," he thought.
"And what if it said, 'Tonight is
Little Owl's Birthday.' And what if there were
signs just like it all over the forest.
Then everyone would know about my birthday!"

"Everyone!" he cried. "That's it!
I'll make signs."

Little Owl ran back to his house.
There he found some boards.

Little Owl put all the boards on the floor.
Then he opened a can of paint. He stuck
one wing into the paint and wrote
on the first board,

"TONIGHT IS LITTLE OWL'S BIRTHDAY."

"I'll put this sign down by the river,"
Little Owl thought. He painted a picture
of some water at the bottom of the sign
to help him remember where it should go.

Then he stuck his other wing into the paint.
"I'll put this sign on the old tree
in the hollow," he said. So he painted
some leaves at the bottom of that sign.

He went on making signs until all the boards
were painted. He painted something
at the bottom of each sign so he would
remember where to put it.

After he had finished the signs, Little Owl
took them and went down the path.

15

When he got to the tree in the hollow,
he remembered that he needed something else.
He left the signs near the bottom of the tree
and ran home to get a hammer and some nails.
When he came back, all the signs were gone.

A Night Full of Surprises

Little Owl could hear someone hammering
down in the hollow. He went down
into the hollow.

The hammering stopped. Mole looked out
from behind a tree. "Is that you, Little Owl?"
he said in his slow, sad way. "It's me — Mole."

"Hello, Mole," said Little Owl. "I haven't
seen you in a long time."

"No one does," said Mole. "But I saw you,
Little Owl. And you have made me very happy."

"I have?" asked Little Owl. "You don't
look happy."

"Oh, I always look like this," said Mole.
"But tonight I am happy. Do you know
what tonight is, Little Owl?"

"I do!" said Little Owl. "Do you know?"

"Tonight is my birthday," said Mole.

"*Your* birthday?" cried Little Owl.

"Every year it's my birthday," Mole went on.
"But no one ever knows. But *you* remembered,
Little Owl."

"I did?" asked Little Owl.

"Yes, you did," Mole went on. "You said
to yourself that tonight must be
Mole's birthday. So you made that present,
Little Owl. You brought it here
and set it down near my hole. Then you ran off
so that I would be surprised. Oh, Little Owl,"
said Mole. "I'm so happy! Come and see."

Mole took Little Owl farther down
into the hollow. "Look!" he said. "My new house.
Isn't it beautiful?"

Little Owl could hardly believe his eyes.
Mole was making a house out of
Little Owl's signs.

"I've always wanted a real house," said Mole.
"And now, I will have one because of
your present. I'll sit in it all day long
and look at the beautiful paintings you made
for me." Mole could not read. In fact,
he could not even see very well.

"Oh, it will be a happy home," said Mole.
"And a happy birthday."

Little Owl looked at his signs. Some of them
were already nailed together. "Now no one
will ever know about my birthday," he said
to himself.

Then Little Owl looked at Mole's happy face.
He got his hammer and helped Mole build
his house.

Mole and Little Owl finished building
Mole's new house. Then they sat down
and looked at the house.

"Do you know what tonight is, Mole?" said
Little Owl. "Tonight is my birthday, too."

"Your birthday and my birthday are
on the same night?" cried Mole.

"That's right," said Little Owl. "Let's go
to my house. Birthdays are more fun if you
share them."

Mole was very happy. He had never
shared his birthday with anyone before.

Little Owl and Mole came out of the hollow
and started down the path. Little Owl said,
"Mole, I will teach you a birthday song."
They sang the birthday song all the way
to Little Owl's house.

They climbed the steps to Little Owl's house
in the Old Tree. Little Owl opened the door.

"Surprise!" everyone shouted.
"Happy birthday, Little Owl!"

Little Owl couldn't believe his eyes.
The kitchen was all lighted up. The table
was set for a party.

Around the table stood Raccoon and Bear,
Old Possum, the gray rabbit and his sister,
and all of Little Owl's friends.

"What's going on, Little Owl?" Mole whispered.

"It's a birthday party!" cried Little Owl.

He ran over to his mother and gave her
a big hug.

"You did remember my birthday! And it's
Mole's birthday, too," said Little Owl.

"Happy birthday, Mole!" said Mrs. Owl.

"Happy birthday, Mole and Little Owl!"
everyone cried.

Then Mrs. Owl brought out a big cake
with HAPPY BIRTHDAY written on it.

Everyone ate cake and laughed together.
Then they all sang songs. Mole and Little Owl
sang their birthday song for everyone.

As they sang, Mole and Little Owl looked
at each other. Each of them was thinking
the same thing. "A birthday is more fun
when it is shared."

Help From Commas

You know that commas can help you understand what you're reading if you make a little pause whenever you come to one.

Read the sentence below:

1. Jane, my sister works at the hospital.

The comma in this sentence helps you to know that Jane is being spoken to.

Now read this sentence:

2. Jane, my sister, works at the hospital.

You know that the commas in this sentence tell you who Jane is.

Let's look at another way in which commas can help you understand what you read. Try to read this sentence:

3. Tom had lobster potatoes some corn bread an orange cake and lemonade for dinner.

How many different foods did Tom have? Did he have corn bread or corn and bread? Did he have an orange and cake or orange cake? You can't tell what he had because commas were not put into that sentence to show you where to make a pause.

Below is the same sentence as Sentence 3. But this time commas have been added. Read the sentence and see how the commas help to make the meaning clearer.

4. Tom had lobster, potatoes, some corn bread, an orange, cake, and lemonade for dinner.

Now can you tell how many different foods Tom had?

If a sentence has in it the names of a lot of things one right after another, look for the commas. Use them to help you know just what the different things are.

Following are pairs of sentences that use the same words but have commas in different places. Use what you know about commas to help you understand the difference in meaning between the two sentences.

5. Mary Ann, Donna, Betty Sue, and Joan are having a yard sale.

6. Mary, Ann, Donna, Betty Sue, and Joan are having a yard sale.

How many people are having a yard sale in Sentence 5? How many in Sentence 6?

7. They are selling candles, paper, hats, food, books, and games.

8. They are selling candles, paper hats, food books, and games.

How many things are they selling in Sentence 7? How many in Sentence 8?

Use what you know about commas
to help you answer the questions below
these sentences.

9. I have a bear, a race car,
    a detective game, and a truck
    in my toy box.

   How many toys are in the toy box?

10. Mark, the boy who lives here has a dog.
11. Mark, the boy who lives here, has a dog.

   In which sentence does Mark have a dog?
   In which sentence is Mark being spoken to?

12. I have my pencil, homework, notebook,
    and library book in my book bag.

   How many things are in the book bag?

Six Special Places

by MONICA De BRUYN

Nora, Peter, and Jill wanted a special place
of their own. So one winter day they made
a house out of snow.

They played in it all winter.

But then spring came. And soon
the snow house had melted away.

"We need a new place," said Nora.

She made a little cave with chairs
and a blanket.

"Let's make it bigger!" said Peter.

They made it so big that it took up
most of the space in Nora's room.

When Mother looked in, she said,
"You must take it down before dinner.
We need to use the chairs."

Then Peter had an idea.

He thought of a place under the trees.
It was a good place on hot days.

But then someone wanted to build a
new house on the lot. Mr. Moss came
and cut down the trees.

Nora, Peter, and Jill needed a new place.

So this time they made a little house
near the brook.

They tied branches together to make
the walls. They put grass over the branches
to make a roof.

But one day while Nora, Peter, and Jill
were away, some people had a picnic
down by the brook. The next morning
the children found the roof caved in.

The next day Jill made a little tent
in the garage.
   Jill, Peter, and Nora sang songs
and played games in the tent until bedtime.
Then they went to sleep feeling happy.

The next morning their father said,
"You will have to take that tent down.
My new workbench is coming today. I'll need
this spot for the workbench."

"But this is our special place!" cried Peter.
"Where can we go now?"

"You can build something else
in another place," said their father. "You can
use some of these boards. I'll let you use
the hammer and give you some nails."

"But where can we build it?" asked Peter.

Nora had an idea.

"Daddy, could we build our very own house
in the back yard?" Nora asked.

"Yes, and I know just the spot for it,"
Daddy said.

Then they all worked together to build
a little house in that spot.

"This is the best place of all," said Jill.
"This time our troubles are over for good."

But the next day, they had a big surprise.
Nora and Peter and Jill weren't the only ones
that liked the little house in the yard.

Busy Carpenters

by JAMES S. TIPPETT

The song of the saw
Is true
As we cut the boards
In two.

The song of the plane
Is sweet
As the shavings curl
At our feet.

And the song of the hammer
Is good
As we drive the nails
In the wood.

Josefina February

by EVALINE NESS

Josefina February lived on a high hill
in Haiti. She lived with her grandfather,
Mr. February.

In front of their house stood a big tree.
In the tree Josefina had her own sitting room.
From her room in the tree, she could watch
the sea and the market place.

In back of their house was a grove of trees.
Many kinds of fruit grew on the trees.
Beautiful flowers grew in the grove, too.

Early every morning Josefina and
her grandfather went to the grove to pick
some fruit. They put the fruit in baskets
to carry on their heads. Then they carried
the fruit down the hill to the market place.
With the money they got from the fruit
they sold, they could buy the things they
needed at home. Mr. February always gave
Josefina a coin or two to use as she pleased.

Josefina loved the market place. There was
so much to see and smell and hear. There were
people, baskets, hats, and ribbons. And they
were all mixed in with fruit, bowls, and shoes.

One morning Josefina and Mr. February
did not go to the market. Mr. February went
to work all day in Mr. Hippolyte's fields.
He told Josefina to play at home — but Josefina
had other plans.

That day was her grandfather's birthday.
Josefina wanted to buy him a pair
of real leather shoes. She decided to go
to the market alone. Maybe she could sell
one basket of fruit. Then she would have
enough money, with the coins she had saved,
to buy the shoes.

After her grandfather left, Josefina took
the basket and went to the grove of trees.
While she was picking the fruit, she heard
a sound. It seemed to come from behind
a bush.

Josefina looked behind the bush and saw
a little black burro. The hair on top
of his head was brown. It was just a fringe
of hair. But it looked like a little cap.
The burro's ears looked as long as his legs.
And his legs were so wobbly he could
hardly stand.

Josefina picked him up and held him close.
The little burro put his ears back
and pushed his head under Josefina's chin.
She decided to call him Cap.

Josefina wondered if Cap belonged to someone.
How she wished he belonged to her! She would
teach him tricks. She would play games
with him. And when he was older, she would
ride on his back to the sea.

Josefina was so busy daydreaming,
she almost forgot about going to the market.
She couldn't bear the thought of leaving Cap.
So she decided to take him with her.

On to the Market

As she stood there in the hot sun, Josefina suddenly felt cold. What if Cap belonged to the very first person she met? Or did it really matter if it was the first person? First person or last person — it would be the same. If Cap belonged to someone else, he couldn't belong to her.

But maybe he was like Josefina. Maybe he had no mother, no father, no sister, and no brother. Cap might not even have a grandfather. He might not belong to anyone in the whole world but Josefina!

Somehow Josefina felt better. So she put her basket on her head, picked up Cap, and started down the hill.

As she walked along, the first person
she met was Lilly. Lilly was the tallest,
but not the friendliest, girl on the hill.

"Pardon me, Lilly," Josefina said. "As you
can see, I have a baby burro here. Does he
belong to you?"

Lilly went by without a word.

When Lilly had gone, Josefina whispered
to Cap, "Well, anyway, it wasn't
the *first* person."

Josefina met no one else until she got
to the bottom of the hill. There she saw
a little girl and her brother selling oranges.
Josefina went up to them and said, "Pardon me.
As you can see, I have a baby burro here.
What do you think of him?"

The girl and her brother said, "We wish
he belonged to us!"

Josefina smiled and walked on along the road.

Just then she heard a loud cackle,
then another, and another. She turned around
and saw an old woman with three blackbirds.

Josefina asked, "Pardon me, have you lost
a baby burro?" The old woman didn't say
a word.

But the three blackbirds cackled,
"Not we! Not we! Not we!"

49

Soon she came to a house that looked like
a kite on a string. There she saw two sisters
named Yvette and Yvonne. Josefina walked up
to them. "Miss Yvette and Miss Yvonne,
would you know anyone who might have lost a
baby burro? This burro here?" she asked.

Yvette and Yvonne smiled at Josefina
and said no.

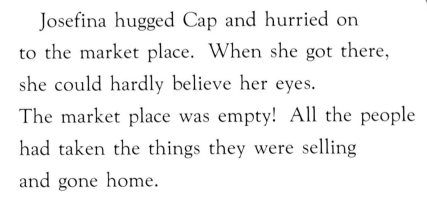

Josefina hugged Cap and hurried on
to the market place. When she got there,
she could hardly believe her eyes.
The market place was empty! All the people
had taken the things they were selling
and gone home.

Josefina didn't know what to do. She was
happy and sad at the same time. Now
Cap belonged to her. But she had not sold
the fruit. And she had no real leather shoes
to give to her grandfather for his birthday.

The Birthday Surprise

Josefina turned away from the market place and started to walk slowly home. As she went by Mr. Hippolyte's fields, she was surprised to hear her name called. It was Mr. Hippolyte.

Josefina tried to smile, but she couldn't. She wanted to tell Mr. Hippolyte her trouble, but right now she couldn't say a word. Mr. Hippolyte just waited. At last Josefina told him her story.

Mr. Hippolyte looked at Josefina a long time. Then he said, "It just so happens that I have a new pair of real leather shoes. Would you be willing to give me Cap for the shoes?"

It was Josefina's turn to look at Mr. Hippolyte a long time. Then she said, "Yes."

While she waited for Mr. Hippolyte to get the shoes, Josefina took the ribbons from her hair. She tied them in Cap's brown hair. She hugged Cap and told him to be good. She promised Cap she would never, never forget him.

When Josefina got home, it was almost dark.
She began to make a birthday supper
for her grandfather.

She had just put the shoes on the table
when Mr. February walked in. He stood there
and smiled at Josefina. And Josefina stood
there and smiled back. Then Mr. February
put on his real leather shoes and
gave Josefina a big hug.

After supper, Mr. February said,
"Poor Mr. Hippolyte. He has a responsibility,
not a very big one. But he thinks he cannot
take care of it alone. He wondered if you
would like to take care of it for him."

Josefina looked at her grandfather.
Mr. Hippolyte had a responsibility! Before she
could say a word, the door slowly opened.

And in wobbled a little black burro. He had
a brown cap of hair with ribbons in it.

The Great Eraser

by ILO ORLEANS

My blackboard was
The soft white sand,
Which stretched out far
On every hand.

I searched and found
An empty shell,
And wrote out words
That I can spell.

But waves dashed on
The sand to play,
And washed my letters
All away.

And that is how
I got the notion —
A great eraser
Is the ocean.

Choosing Correct Meanings

Many words have more than one meaning.
When you see the word <u>bowl</u> written by
itself, you cannot tell if the word means
a dish or to play a game with a ball.
But if the word <u>bowl</u> is in a sentence,
the other words in the sentence will help
you to know which meaning to use.

Think about the meaning the word <u>bowl</u>
has in each sentence below.

1. When Mother went to the kitchen, she got
   a **bowl** to put the apples in.
2. When Mother went out to **bowl** with her
   friends, she forgot to take her ball.

In which sentence does <u>bowl</u> mean a dish?
What words in the sentence helped you
to know that?

In which sentence does <u>bowl</u> mean to play
a game? What words in the sentence
helped you to know that?

Now read the sentences below. Each word in heavy black letters has more than one meaning. Use the other words in the sentence to help you decide which meaning the word has in each sentence.

3. She didn't hear the doorbell **ring.**
4. She has a new **ring** on her finger.

In which sentence does ring mean to make a noise? What words in the sentence helped you to know that?

5. We found a rubber elephant in an old **trunk** in the garage.
6. An elephant uses its **trunk** to get food to its mouth.

In which sentence does trunk mean a part of an elephant's body? What words in the sentence helped you to know that?

Sometimes in your reading you may come to a word for which you know only one meaning. But the meaning you know does not make sense in the sentence you are reading. Thinking about the other words in the sentence may help you to learn another meaning for that word.

You know that the word <u>duck</u> means a bird. Try that meaning in this sentence.

7. We had to **duck** our heads to keep from getting hit by the ball.

In reading this sentence, you knew that the word <u>duck</u> could not mean a bird.

The other words in the sentence helped you to know that <u>duck</u> probably means to move in some way to keep from getting hit by something. The other words in the sentence helped you to learn a new meaning for the word <u>duck</u>.

Read the sentences below. The meaning
of each word in heavy black letters may be
new to you. Use the other words in
the sentence to help you find the meaning
for that word.

8. After a long time, they opened the doors
   so we could **board** the boat and go
   to New York.

   Does <u>board</u> in this sentence mean a piece
of wood or to get on? What words helped you
to know that?

9. It stayed light for a long time tonight,
   because the sun did not **set** until after
   nine o'clock.

   Does <u>set</u> in this sentence mean to place
something somewhere or to go down?
What words helped you to know that?

   When you do not know the meaning
of a word you read in a sentence,
the other words in the sentence
may help you to find a meaning.

Have You Ever Seen . . .

a fish bowl?

a horse fly?

a sleeping bag?

a shoe box?

a walking stick?

a bed spring?

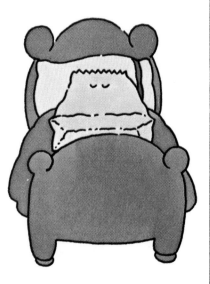

A Mouthful of Words

Read these sentences out loud three times. Each time read the sentence faster than the time before.

The small sleepy squirrel shouted shoo at the shy scared sheep.

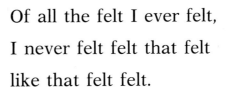

Of all the felt I ever felt,
I never felt felt that felt
like that felt felt.

The brave black bee bit
the busy brown bear
because the brave black bee
believed the busy brown bear
was breakfast.

Fun With a Hobby

Look at the pictures below. Which of these things do you do?

Sometimes you do things because you must do them. Sometimes you do things because you like to do them.

You may have one thing that you like to do very much. It is something you have fun doing when you have the time. It may be your hobby.

The pictures on the next pages show some people and their hobbies.

Some people may make a hobby
of collecting things.

What other things could
someone collect?

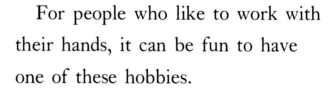

For people who like to work with
their hands, it can be fun to have
one of these hobbies.

What other things could
someone make?

For some people these kinds of things are fun.

Have you ever done any of these kinds of things?

For some people, sports and games make good hobbies.

What are some other sports and games that would make good hobbies?

Hobbies can be interesting and fun.

The String Collection

by MARY RADLOFF

Mr. Fergus was a collector. He collected bottles with pretty shapes and boxes of all sizes. He collected rocks of many colors and seashells from the beaches of the world.

One day as Mr. Fergus was walking down Main Street in the town of Sunnyvale, he found a piece of string. It was short and strong. It was a lovely shade of red. Mr. Fergus picked it up.

"This," said Mr. Fergus to himself, "is the beginning of my string collection!"

He wound the piece of red string into a ball and put it in his pocket. Mr. Fergus stopped at the meat market for a pound of meat for supper. He was pleased to see the man tie the package with a piece of white string.

When Mr. Fergus got home, he pulled the white string off the package. He tied one end to the end of his ball of red string and wound it carefully around. The ball of string was now a little larger.

Mr. Fergus put the ball in a special box and wrote on the box the words "String Collection."

Every day Mr. Fergus added to his string collection. He bought new shoes. The woman at the store tied the box with soft brown string. Mr. Fergus tied the brown string to the end of his collection and wound it around. The ball grew larger.

He bought three shirts at the store and carried them home by the strong green string around the package. He tied the end of the green string to his collection and wound it around. The ball grew larger.

A few times the newspaper carrier ran out of rubber bands and tied Mr. Fergus's paper with blue string. Mr. Fergus tied the blue string to his collection. The ball grew larger.

One day the letter carrier brought a book. The package was tied with soft black string. Mr. Fergus tied the black string to his collection and wound it around. The ball grew larger.

Soon Mr. Fergus's string collection was so large
it would no longer fit in the box. He moved it to a
table in the kitchen. One night the big ball rolled
right off the table. It made a loud bumping noise,
and Mr. Fergus had to get out of bed to see what
was wrong. After that, he just left the collection
on the floor.

When spring came, Mr. Fergus could just roll
the large ball of string through the kitchen door
and out into the back yard. It looked bright and
colorful there with the grass showing green
around it. A few flowers added a red color of
their own along the fence.

Soon the children of Sunnyvale learned of Mr. Fergus's string collection. They began to bring him string from lunch bags, string from old games, and string they found in boxes at home.

The string collection grew so large that Mr. Fergus had to use his ladder to get to the top of the ball to tie and wind more string. He was so busy tying and winding he had no time at all for collecting bottles, boxes, rocks, or shells from the beaches of the world.

Now the ball of string was so large it filled his whole back yard. He had no room for flowers, no room for grass.

The ball of string was so large it shaded his kitchen window and made the room dark.

"This is enough!" cried Mr. Fergus at the end of one long day of tying and winding string.

"I am through collecting string. I am through tying and winding. I want my yard back with green grass and flowers. I am no longer a collector of strings!"

Mr. Fergus felt much better after that, but he
still had one problem. He still had a yard full of
a ball of string. It was too big to carry. It was
too heavy to move. It was too large to roll. How
would he ever get rid of such a large collection
of string?

Mr. Fergus thought and thought. At last a slow smile came over his face. Mr. Fergus had a good idea! He went into his house and was very busy with paper, sticks, ribbons, and even some string. He sang as he worked, and a few times he laughed to himself. He went to bed that night a happy man.

The next day was sunny. Mr. Fergus did nothing.

The day after that was rainy. Mr. Fergus did nothing.

Then the day after that was windy. Mr. Fergus went out carrying the paper-stick-ribbon-string-thing he had made. He tied one end of it to the end of his string collection. It looked a little like — very much like it — like it was a kite!

Mr. Fergus waited for a good strong wind, and then he threw the kite into the air. It swished and pulled. It danced and climbed. As the kite went up, it took with it Mr. Fergus's string collection. As the kite went higher, the ball of string grew smaller.

The children of Sunnyvale came to watch. All morning, all afternoon, on into the early evening, they watched. The ball of string disappeared as the kite disappeared. At last both the kite and the collection were gone forever.

"Hooray!" shouted the children.

Just then the wind left a little feather at the feet
of Mr. Fergus.

"Hmmmmm," said Mr. Fergus as he picked it
up. "This is the beginning of my new collection!"

My Kite

by MYRA COHN LIVINGSTON

It was splendid,
my kite —
It flew and it flew
When we let out the string
In the wind,
And we knew

   It would fly with the birds —
   It would fly to the sea —

Then its tail
Tangled up in a
Terrible tree.

Books to Enjoy

Bullfrog Builds a House by Rosamond Dauer

Bullfrog's friend Gertrude helps him build
a house. When the house is finished, Bullfrog
sees that it needs one thing more.

Let's Make a Deal by Linda Glovach

Can two boys share a dog? They can until one
of the boys has to move away.

A Bargain for Frances by Russell Hoban

Frances shows how bright she is when her friend
tries to play a trick on her.

The Surprise Party by Annabelle Prager

When Nicky plans his own birthday party,
it really turns out to be a surprise party.

Fish Out of School by Evelyn Shaw

A fish lost at sea faces many problems as she
tries to find her friends.

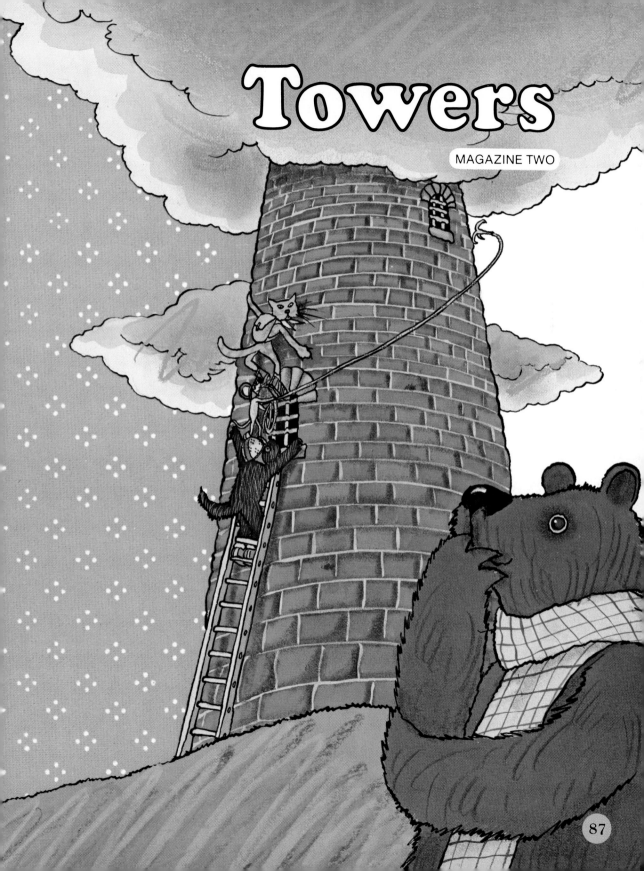

Towers

MAGAZINE TWO

Contents

The Brave Baby Sitter

by BARBARA GREENBERG

The doorbell rang, and Lisa ran over
to open the door. It was Heather, Lisa's
favorite baby sitter. Heather came in
and said, "Hi, Lis. You got a haircut! Now
I can see your neck. And I can tickle it
right here!"

Lisa laughed. She always had
a good time with Heather. Heather
liked to read books out loud. She
laughed hard at the silly parts.
And she changed her voice
for the scary parts. She was
good at making things, and she
called Lisa "Lis".

Mother left, and Lisa and Heather got
to work on a collage. Lisa liked to paste
all kinds of things together. They used
bright-colored paper, ribbons, and pieces
of string. They even used some buttons.
They used silver and brown buttons and
a big shiny gold one.

It started raining while they were working
on the collage. It was a strong, windy rain.
It beat against the house and rattled
the windows.

Suddenly the darkness outside got white
with light. Then they heard a crashing sound.

"Oh, no," said Heather. "Thunder!"
She dropped a button and held onto the chair.
"Get ready. Here comes another one," she said
when she saw the lightning again.

"What's wrong, Heather?" asked Lisa.
"Are you scared?"

"Scared? Who's scared of a little thunder?"
said Heather when it was quiet again. "Now
listen, you thunder, you'll have to whisper,
please!" she shouted.

Lisa laughed.

"Oh, no. Here comes more," said Heather.
This time she put her hands over her ears
and shut her eyes tight.

Lisa said, "My mother always tells me
to keep busy so I don't think so much
about the thunder. So let's paste."

Lisa pasted her buttons and ribbons
and pieces of string on some paper.
She loved sticking her fingers in the paste
and making collages. She didn't think
about the thunder.

But Heather was thinking about the thunder and *not* about what she was doing. She pasted a picture right onto the table instead of onto the paper.

"Oh, no," said Heather when she saw what she had done.

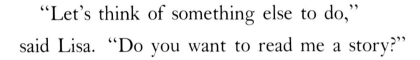

"Let's think of something else to do,"
said Lisa. "Do you want to read me a story?"

Lisa and Heather snuggled together
in the big soft chair in the living room.
Heather began to read a story. Then came
a flash of lightning and a crash of thunder.
Heather pulled Lisa closer to her.

Heather went on reading. But she didn't
laugh now at the silly parts or change
her voice for the scary parts. She read
and then looked out of the window. Then she
read again and looked out of the window again.
She kept losing her place.

There was another flash of light. Then *crash* went the thunder!

"That was a loud one," said Heather.

"It will stop soon," said Lisa.

"You're brave, Lis," said Heather.

Then Lisa said, "Let's draw with crayons."

Lisa drew a picture of a sunny day. She drew red and yellow flowers and a big, round, orange sun. Heather drew a picture of a rainy day with a flash of lightning across the sky.

"I like yours better," said Heather.

"Here," said Lisa. "I made it for you."

Soon it was Lisa's bedtime. When Lisa
got ready for bed, Heather said, "You may
stay up tonight until the rain stops.
Let's stay together a little while longer."

"Sometimes when there's thunder outside,
my mother puts on some music and we dance,"
Lisa said.

Lisa and Heather put on some music and turned
it up loud. Heather loved to dance. She and Lisa
danced all around the room.

When the music stopped, Heather said,
"Look, it's stopped raining. There's
no more thunder."

"I'd better go to bed now," said Lisa.

"You're a very brave baby sitter, Lis,"
said Heather. "I forgot all about
the thunder."

"I know," said Lisa. "I hope there's thunder
the next time you come. Then I can take care
of you again. I like being a baby sitter."

Go Wind

by LILIAN MOORE

Go wind, blow
Push wind, swoosh.
    Shake things
    take things
    make things
        fly.

    Ring things
    swing things
    fling things
        high.

Go wind, blow
Push things — whee.
    No, wind, no.
    Not me —
    not *me*.

Following Directions

Below are some directions for making an alligator. To make the alligator, you will need scissors, a piece of green paper, and a pencil.

When you read directions, you must read very carefully. First read through all of the directions so that you will better understand what you are to do. Then you are ready to follow the directions one by one.

1. Fold the green paper in half the long way.

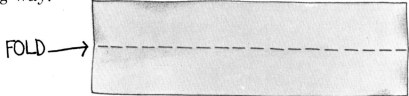

FOLD →

2. Now draw an alligator, using the folded side for the alligator's back.

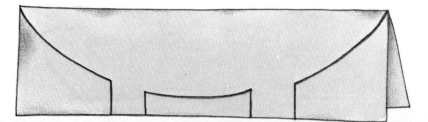

3. Keep the paper folded and cut along
   the lines you have drawn. <u>Do</u> <u>not</u> cut
   the fold.

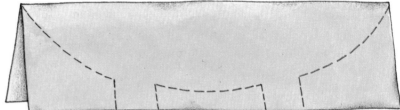

4. Keep your paper folded. Cut about six
   small slits in the folded side as shown
   below. Don't put slits too close to the
   parts that will be the alligator's head
   and tail.

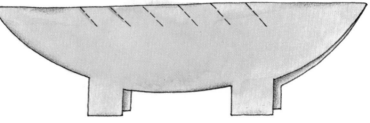

5. Next unfold your alligator and fold back
   the slits like this:

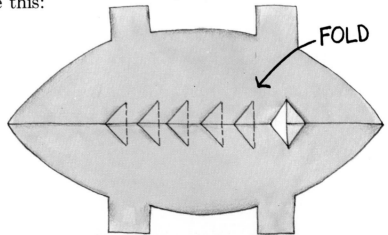

FOLD

6. Now fold the alligator together again. Draw an eye on each side.

7. If you want your alligator to show its teeth, cut out the mouth like this:

When you read directions, try to understand clearly just what things you are to do and in what order you are to do them.

It's Hard to Believe

People in the Play

Storyteller	**Luis**
Man	**Ana**
Woman	**Clever Marta**

Scene One

On the road to the market

Storyteller: Long ago, on a road far from here, a man, a woman, and a donkey were walking to town. The man was leading the donkey by a rope.

Now there was nothing strange about the man and nothing strange about the woman. But there was something *very* strange about the donkey.

Storyteller: Most donkeys have big ears that stick *up*.
This donkey had little ears that stuck *out*.

Most donkeys have straight tails that
hang *down*. This donkey had a curly tail
that stuck *out*.

Yes, this donkey was one funny-looking animal.

On this day, the man and the woman were
going to the market place. As they walked
along, they talked about what they had
to buy there.

Woman: It's a good thing we have our donkey.
We'll have a lot to carry home today.

Storyteller: The man and the woman were
busy talking. They didn't see
the two strangers who were sitting
under the bushes watching them.
The two strangers were Ana and Luis.

Luis: Look at that donkey! Have you ever seen
such a funny-looking animal?

Ana: No, never! But funny as he looks, I wish
he were ours. We could sell him and make
a lot of money.

Luis: I hadn't thought of that! I wish we knew a way to get that donkey. Let's try to think of a way.

Storyteller: Ana and Luis sat and thought. After a while, Ana jumped up!

Ana: I have it! I have a plan to get the donkey. Hurry! Let's follow that woman and that man.

Storyteller: As they hurried along, Ana told Luis what her plan was. Soon they saw the man and the woman up ahead of them.

Luis: There they are! I can see them now!

Ana: *(Whispering)* Sh! We don't want them to hear us.

Storyteller: When they were behind the donkey, Luis quickly took the rope off the donkey's neck. Then he put the rope around his own neck. Ana hid the donkey behind some bushes. The woman and the man were still busy talking. They didn't see or hear a thing. They just kept on walking and talking.

Man: I'm getting tired. Let's rest here
for a few minutes.

Woman: All right. But not for —

Storyteller: The woman's eyes opened wide.
She put her hands over her mouth. The man
looked around and he saw what had surprised
the woman. He saw Luis where his donkey
had been.

Man: Who are *you?*

Woman: And where is our donkey?

Luis: I know you're surprised. But I *am* your donkey!

Man: Don't try to fool us! We know you're not a donkey!

Woman: We can see that you're a man!

Luis: Let me explain. You see, first I *was* a man. Then I was changed into a donkey. Now I've been changed back into a man. Isn't that wonderful?

Woman: Your story is hard to believe! Still, you *are* tied with the same rope that our donkey was tied with. I don't know what to think!

Man: Well, our donkey is gone, and this man is here. I guess we have to believe him, but what do we do with him now?

Luis: Why don't you tell everyone I'm your donkey?

Woman: What? Why, that's silly. Everyone would laugh at us. I don't want people laughing at us!

Man: Yes, people will laugh if we say a man is our donkey. Take that rope off your neck and get away from us.

Woman: Yes, hurry! I don't want anyone to see you with us!

Luis: All right, I'll leave if you really want me to.

Storyteller: The man and woman started again on their way to town. Meanwhile, Luis went back to the place where Ana was waiting with the donkey.

Ana: Did you do it? Did you fool them?

Luis: Yes, fooling them was easy. Now I'll wait here while you go into town and sell the donkey.

Ana: That's a good idea. We don't want the woman and the man to see you again.

Scene Two

At the Market Place

Storyteller: The man and the woman decided not to buy very much at the market. Now that they no longer had their donkey, they would have to carry everything home themselves.

Woman: We'd better not buy anything else. We can't carry any more.

Man: You're right. If you carry this bag, then I'll take —

Storyteller: Just then the man saw Ana with the donkey.

Man: Look! Look at that woman trying to sell that funny-looking donkey. I've never seen her before, but doesn't that look like our donkey?

Woman: It *must* be our donkey. There could never be another donkey so funny-looking! But how can we prove it?

Man: Let's go and ask Clever Marta. She'll help us.

Storyteller: Now Clever Marta was
the wisest person in town. People came
to her with their problems, and she always
helped them. She listened as the man
and the woman told her what had happened.

Clever Marta: That's a very strange story,
but don't worry. I know how you can prove
that this woman has your donkey.

Storyteller: By this time Ana had seen the man
and the woman. And she knew they had seen
her. Oh, how she wished she'd taken
the donkey to a different market!

Then she heard Clever Marta calling her.

Clever Marta: You! Please come here.
But leave that donkey where he is.

Storyteller: By now everyone in the market was watching them. Ana had to do what Clever Marta told her.

Clever Marta: These people say that you have their donkey. Is that true?

Ana: Of course not. That is my donkey!

Clever Marta: All right. If that is your donkey, call him to you.

Ana: Oh, all right. Uh, . . . Come, Slow Boy. . . . No, I mean Short Ears. . . . Oh, you ugly donkey! . . . That's it! Come, Ugly!

Storyteller: Ana called the donkey by
many different names, but the donkey
didn't move. Then Clever Marta turned
to the man.

Clever Marta: Now *you* call the donkey.

Man: Come, Beautiful One! Come here!

Storyteller: The donkey lifted his ears,
looked at the man and the woman,
and came at once.

Clever Marta: Look, the donkey knows his real name. Now we know who the donkey really belongs to.

Man: We have our donkey back. And we have you to thank for helping us, Clever Marta.

Clever Marta: Tell me something. Your donkey is so funny-looking. Why do you call him Beautiful One?

Woman: We know he's funny-looking, but he is our helper. And that makes him beautiful to us.

Storyteller: The man turned to his donkey.

Man: I don't know how you got changed back into a donkey. I am just glad that we're all back together again.

Child of the Navajos

by SEYMOUR REIT

Bobby Cohoe is a Navajo Indian boy.
Bobby is growing up in two worlds. He is
a modern American boy. And at the same time,
he is a child of the Navajos.

Bobby lives on the Navajo Reservation
in Arizona with his father, his mother,
and his little sister.

Bobby's home is high up on Black Mesa.
A mesa is a hill with a flat top. There are
many mesas on the reservation.

Many Navajos own cattle and sheep.
Bobby's father owns cattle, sheep, and goats.

Bobby goes to Rough Rock School.
Most of the children in his school come
from far away. They live at Rough Rock School
all week. On weekends the children go back
to their own homes.

Bobby's teacher and the children in his class
can speak Navajo.

Here is a sentence in Navajo:

Shimá éí ajidiz dooleeł, diyogí jidootł'óół biniiyé.

Here is the same sentence in English:

My mother is busy spinning, so she can weave a rug.

Bobby's class is learning to speak, read,
and write English. They are learning
arithmetic and drawing, too.

The teacher tells the children
some of the old Navajo stories. She sings
the old Navajo songs for them.

From the older men, the children learn
Navajo dances. These dances have been done
by the Navajo people for hundreds of years.

At Rough Rock there are
special School Mothers and
School Fathers. They live
at school and help
to take care of the boys
and girls.

Bobby's School Mother
shows the children how
to make a special kind
of bread. It is called fry bread
because it is fried in a pan.

She shows them how to spin,
too. She spins wool to make
beautiful things.

Bobby's School Father
tells the children stories
of the Navajos. He tells them
of times, long ago, when
the Navajos were hunters.

On Friday, Bobby's father comes to Rough Rock
to take him home for the weekend.

For many years the family rode in a wagon.
The wagon was pulled by a horse. But now
Bobby's father has a new truck to drive.
Little by little, the old ways are changing.

Bobby at Home

When Bobby is at home, he helps
to take care of the sheep and cattle.

At sunset, the sheep are put
inside a big pen. This keeps them safe
at night.

On Saturday, Bobby likes to go
to the store with his family. They
must drive a long way to get there.

This is Bobby's uncle. He is a silversmith.
Bobby likes to watch his uncle cut and work
the shining silver.

In the winter, Bobby's family lives
in a small, wooden house. But when winter
is over, the family moves to another house
called a hogan. A hogan is made
of hard mud and wood. Many Navajo people
live in hogans year round. At one time,
the Navajo people all lived in hogans.

Spring is picnic time. On Sundays,
Bobby's family and their friends
sometimes go on a picnic. They go to a place
where there was once an old Indian well.
It is called *To ha ha diee,* and it means,
"Place where the water is drawn."

After the picnic food is eaten,
Bobby and his friends have fun playing games
and sliding down the hills.

Sometimes Bobby goes
for a walk all by himself.
He likes to climb the rocks
and walk among the trees.

When he is by himself, Bobby thinks
about the Navajo people.

He remembers what his grandfather
once told him. His grandfather said that
the Navajos will go on and on, "as long
as the rivers shall run and the grass shall grow."

Sometimes Bobby likes to sit and think
about his people. He wants very much to be
a Navajo like his father and his grandfather.
He knows that some day, like them,
he will be grown up.

He knows that some day he will
do the Navajo dances with the other men.

This he knows, for he is an Indian boy.

This he knows, for he is Bobby Cohoe, an
American and a child of the Navajos.

What Is Different?

Look at these two pictures. They look the same, but they are different. There are five things that are different in the two pictures. Can you find them all?

Words In Alphabetical Lists

Suppose you wanted to find the word <u>hop</u> in a list that had three words. It would be easy to read through the three words until you found the word <u>hop</u>.

But suppose you were looking for the word <u>hop</u> in a list that had hundreds of words. With so many words, it would take much longer to find the word <u>hop</u>.

That is why often in books that have lists of words, the words are placed in alphabetical order. Words that begin with the letter <u>a</u> come first, words that begin with the letter <u>b</u> come next, and so on.

day

hurry

hop

late

like

sister

summer

To find a word quickly in an alphabetical
list, you need to know two things. First
you need to know the alphabet. Then you
need to know how to use the alphabet.

A B C D E F G H I J K L M N
O P Q R S T U V W X Y Z

Suppose you came to the word <u>day</u> when
you were looking for the word <u>hop</u>
in an alphabetical list of words. Do you
think you would find <u>hop</u> before <u>day</u>
or after <u>day</u>?

You know that you would find <u>hop</u>
after <u>day</u> because the letter <u>h</u> comes after
the letter <u>d</u> in the alphabet.

A B C (D) E F G (H)

What if you came to a word that began with the same letter as the word you were trying to find? Suppose you were looking for the word <u>hop</u> and you came to the word <u>hurry</u>. Now you have to think about the alphabetical order of the *second* letter.

The second letter of <u>hurry</u> is <u>u</u>. The second letter of <u>hop</u> is <u>o</u>. Does <u>o</u> come before or after <u>u</u> in the alphabet?

M N O P Q R S T U

You know that <u>o</u> comes before <u>u</u> in the alphabet. So the word <u>hop</u> should come before <u>hurry</u>, shouldn't it?

Now suppose you were looking for the word <u>like</u> and you came to the word <u>late</u>. Do you think you would find <u>like</u> before <u>late</u> or after <u>late</u>?

Would you find the word <u>sister</u> before <u>summer</u> or after <u>summer</u>?

138

Following are five lists of words. Look at the first list. The word <u>eye</u> is in heavy black letters. Below the word <u>eye</u> are four words in alphabetical order. Where would you put the word <u>eye</u> if you were adding it to the list?

Do the other four lists the same way. Look at the word in heavy black letters. Decide where you would put that word if you were adding it to the list.

eye	**both**	**chair**	**feed**	**ten**
bed	bear	came	cow	cook
duck	big	clue	far	cut
glad	but	code	fish	note
pig	by	cry	girl	very

The Night the Lights Went Out

by JOHANNA HURWITZ

It was late in the afternoon. Nora was in her bedroom playing. Teddy was washing his hands, and Mom was making dinner. Daddy would be home soon. Suddenly the lights went out.

"Mom," Nora called. "The light went out!"

"Mom," Teddy shouted, "I can't see anything."

Mom came from the kitchen. "The kitchen light is out, too," she said. "The power must be off."

Nora ran to the window and looked out. "Mom," she called. "Come here! Everyone is looking out of their windows."

Teddy and Mom came running. From almost every window in the buildings across the street, people were looking out.

Mom opened the window. The cold air came into the room.

"What's happened?" called a voice from across the street.

"There must be a power failure," Mom called back.

"What's a power failure?" Nora asked as her mother closed the window.

"It means there is something wrong with the electricity. It's getting dark. I had better find some candles."

Mom found the candles. By then, it had gotten very dark in the apartment. Soon she had two candles burning in the kitchen. They gave a small light.

"Now we're all set until the power comes back on," Mom said.

Teddy didn't say anything. He looked scared.

"Teddy," Mom said, "what a lucky night this is. Tonight we're going to live like people lived long ago."

"How was that?" asked Teddy.

"Well, first of all, we're going to have dinner by candlelight."

"I need more light than two candles!" said Teddy.

"I'll light more candles, Teddy," said Mom. "It will be a lot of fun. And Daddy should be here very soon."

She looked at the kitchen clock. The hands hadn't moved. It still said five o'clock.

"Look," said Mom. "The hands on the clock aren't moving. They won't move until the electricity is back on."

Nora was back at the window. The street was dark. There were no lights at all.

"Mom," she said. "All the street lights are out, too."

In the windows across the street, they could see candles burning. They could see people using flashlights, too.

"This is fun," cried Nora.

Mom went back to the kitchen. Teddy went with her.

Mom was lighting another candle when she heard a noise at the door.

"Who is it?" called Mom.

"It's me," a voice answered. "I can't find my key." It was Daddy.

Mom opened the door.

"I had to walk up the stairs," Daddy puffed. "The elevator isn't running.

"It's lucky that I was almost home when the lights went out. The whole west side of the city is dark."

Suddenly Nora thought of something. "If Daddy is home already, it means that I missed my TV show."

"There won't be any TV until the electricity comes back on," said Daddy. "There is no TV or much of anything else without electricity."

"What about the phone?" asked Mom. "I must call Grandfather. He may be worried."

"And you should call Mrs. Waldman," said Daddy. "See if she is all right and if she has any candles."

"The phone is out, too," said Mom.

"I'll take a flashlight and go upstairs to Mrs. Waldman's," said Daddy.

"Ask her to come and have dinner with us," said Mom. "She could even sleep here if she wants. And maybe you should look in on Mrs. Beltz. She's all alone, too."

Daddy took the flashlight. He put a few candles in his pocket before he left.

Dinner was ready when Daddy came back. He
was alone. "Mrs. Waldman and Mrs. Beltz took
the candles," said Daddy. "And they said to thank
you for asking them to come down. But they
didn't want to walk down the dark stairs. They're
going to stay in Mrs. Waldman's apartment."

The family sat down around the kitchen table.
There was cold chicken, vegetables, and rolls.
Mom put little birthday candles in the rolls.

"Can we make a wish even if it isn't our birthday?" asked Nora.

"Why not?" asked Mom.

"I know what I'm going to wish for," said Daddy. "Lights!"

"Will you read to us?" Teddy asked Mom after dinner.

"Yes. I mean no," said Mom. "It's too dark. You'll have to go right off to bed. No stories tonight, and you'll have to go to bed without taking a bath."

"I don't want to put on my pajamas," Teddy said. "And I don't want to go to sleep in the dark."

"You always sleep in the dark," said Nora. "And when you close your eyes, it's dark anyway."

"But when I open them, there's some light. It's never dark like this," said Teddy.

"I have an idea," said Mom. "Just for tonight, you and Nora can go to bed with your clothes on. Just remember to take your shoes off."

Both Teddy and Nora loved the idea. "Let's go to bed right away," shouted Nora.

Mom held the flashlight while Nora got into bed. "Good night," Mom said. She gave Nora a kiss. "In the morning the lights should be working fine again."

"And the TV," said Nora.

Then Mom went with Teddy to his room. She held the flashlight while Teddy got into bed. "Good night," she said and she gave him a kiss. "In the morning the lights will be on again."

Soon the children were asleep in the dark.
They were still asleep when the lights went on
later. Daddy came into their rooms and turned
off their lights.

In the morning Mom asked Nora to change
into clean clothes for school.

"But I'm already dressed," said Nora.

"You're still dressed for Tuesday," said Mom.
"Now it's Wednesday."

When they were eating breakfast, Nora saw that the kitchen clock showed the wrong time. Before she left for work, Mom changed the time on the clock.

Nora wondered about what happened to the time that got lost. "It was never six o'clock or seven o'clock or . . ." she said. "All that time got lost in the dark."

"No," said Daddy. "Tuesday night didn't get lost. You will remember it for a *long* time."

City

by LANGSTON HUGHES

In the morning the city
Spreads its wings
Making a song
In stone that sings.

In the evening the city
Goes to bed
Hanging lights
About its head.

I Like
to Swing

by REGINA SAURO

I start slow

With lazy pushes

And before I know it

I'm clear above the bushes.

Higher and higher, swing wide,

Feels like I have some wings inside!

Then up above the treetops, oh, so high!

At last I'm really sailing, sailing through the sky!

Lions in the Grass

by PHYLLIS S. BUSCH

Do you know that there may be lions
in the grass all around you? Yellow lions
with green teeth? But these lions do not roar
and they cannot walk. These lions are plants.
They are called dandelions.

Dandelions grow all over — in the country
and in the city. You may find them growing
on a playground or by a wall. You may
even find them growing out of a crack
in the sidewalk where there is hardly
any soil.

You might see dandelion blossoms almost any time of the year. But you can find the most dandelions in May and June. On a bright spring day, you can see dandelions shining everywhere. They look like hundreds of little suns.

When it is cloudy or when it is raining, the flowers close up until the sun comes out again.

A dandelion is not just one blossom
but many blossoms together. Each yellow
part is a little flower by itself. It is
called a floret. When you hold one dandelion
in your hand, you are really holding a whole
bunch of flowers.

Then one day the yellow blossoms are gone.
In their place is a fluffy gray ball. If you
blow on this ball, little pieces of fluff
will fly away.

Each bit of fluff has a little seed
with a point on it. Each seed, together
with the fluffy part, is called
a dandelion fruit.

When the wind blows, it picks up
many of the fruits and carries them away.
Some of the fruits land with their
sharp points in the soil. From these fruits,
dandelions grow.

Soon the rain falls. Sometimes it rains
hard. The dandelion fruit stays in place
in the soil.

Water begins to get into the seed and
helps it grow. The first thing to grow out
of the seed is a root. The root grows bigger
and bigger as it goes down into the ground.
Little leaves begin to come up above the ground.

In a few days, green stalks begin to come up from the soil. There are green buds at the ends of the stalks. Inside these buds are the dandelion flowers.

One sunny day the buds open. Once more you can see yellow dandelion flowers everywhere you look.

Butterfly, butterfly, butterfly, butterfly,

Oh look, see it hovering among the flowers,

It is like a baby trying to walk

    and not knowing how to go . . .

            Acoma Indian Song

A little yellow cricket

At the roots of the corn

Is hopping about and singing.

            Papago Indian Song

Sylvester
The Mouse With the Musical Ear

by ADELAIDE HOLL

Sylvester was a country mouse. He lived
in a grassy meadow with lovely sounds
all about him.

On the north was a little road where birds
fluttered and made little chirping sounds.
On the south was a lovely woods
where the meadow larks sang.

On the east was a wheat field
where soft winds made music all day
and crickets chirped all night.

And on the west was a silver brook
that gurgled with a musical beat.

Sylvester was a mouse with a musical ear.
He loved the meadow sounds by day.
He loved the meadow sounds by night.

    He would sit in his doorway, listening
to the birds and to the crickets.

    He would sit, listening to the winds
and to the brook.

    He would sit, humming softly to himself.

One day workers came from the city.
They dug up the little road on the north
and made a big highway.

Now birds no longer fluttered and made
little chirping sounds.

Cars went by ZOOM!

Trucks went by WHOOSH!

Sylvester no longer heard the music
of the birds.

Soon, down the big highway, the city began
to come closer. One day workers came
and cut down the lovely woods on the south.
They put up rows and rows of houses.

Now the meadow larks no longer sang
in the woods. The meadow larks went away
to sing in another place.

The city came closer and closer.
Workers came once more. They cut down
the wheat field on the east and put up rows
and rows of shops. The crickets went away
to chirp in another wheat field. And Sylvester
could no longer hear the soft winds
making music all day.

The city came closer and closer. Workers
came again. They dug up the silver brook
on the west. Now it no longer gurgled
with a musical beat.

Sylvester no longer sat in his doorway
humming softly to himself. He just sat,
listening to the ZOOM of the cars
and the WHOOSH of the trucks.

One day workers came with a big bulldozer.
They dug up the grassy meadow. They dug up
Sylvester's house. They even dug up Sylvester!

"I am no longer a country mouse. I am
a city mouse," he said. "I shall find
another home." And away he went.

Sylvester Finds a New Home

There were many places in the city.
But no place was just right for a mouse
with a musical ear. Some places were
too noisy. And some places were too quiet.
Sylvester went on and on.

All at once he heard lovely sounds. He heard
lovely music. Sylvester went into a place
filled with musical sounds. It was a music shop.
A music shop is just the right place
for a mouse with a musical ear.

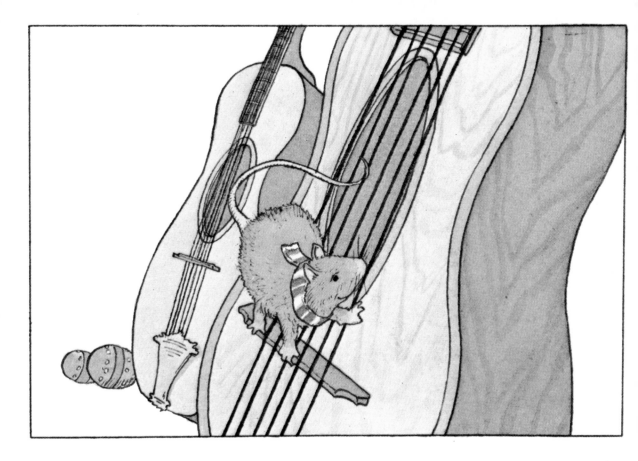

In the music shop, Sylvester saw a fine house
with a little door for going in and coming out.
Across the doorway was a wire fence.
Sylvester went in and sat humming softly
to himself.
    Sylvester liked his house. He liked
the lovely music. Sylvester liked his doorway.
He liked going in and coming out.
When he went across the wire fence, it made
lovely musical sounds.

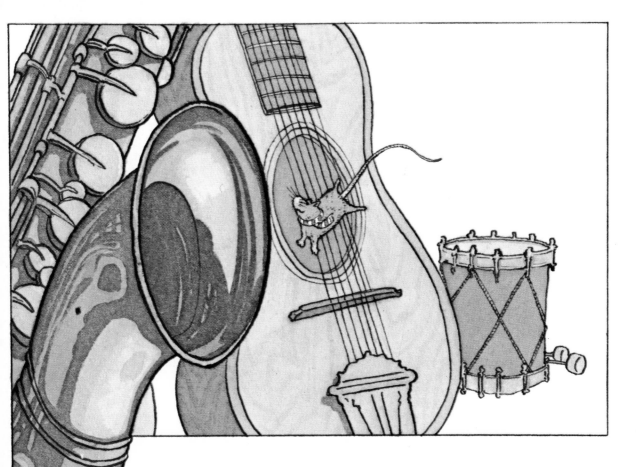

Sylvester was quiet by day. But at night,
when the shop was dark, he played
on the wire fence across his doorway.

He played quiet music.

He played noisy music.

He played the music he heard all day.

People went by the shop at night. "Who is
playing?" they asked. "Who plays lovely music
in your shop at night?" they asked
the shopkeeper.

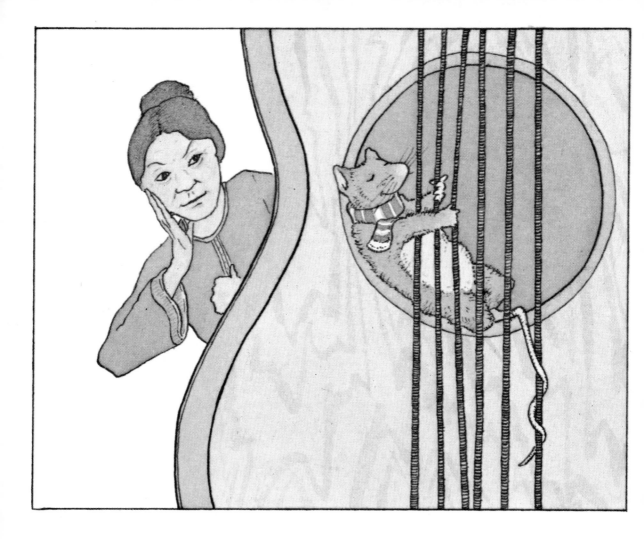

One night the shopkeeper listened
in the dark. Sylvester came softly
to his door. He began to play.

The shopkeeper heard the music. It came
from the guitar on the shelf. But in the dark,
she did not see Sylvester.

"It's a magic guitar!" she cried.
"A magic guitar that plays by itself."

Soon people heard about the magic guitar.
They stood outside the shop at night
and listened.

They went inside the shop by day
and looked. But nobody would buy the guitar.
Nobody needed the magic guitar that played
by itself.

A Friend for Sylvester

Far away in another town, Pete heard
about the magic guitar. Pete loved music,
and he loved to sing. But Pete did not have
a guitar. "A guitar is just what I need,"
he said. "A magic guitar that plays
by itself!"

Pete traveled a long, long way.
He traveled along, singing as he went.

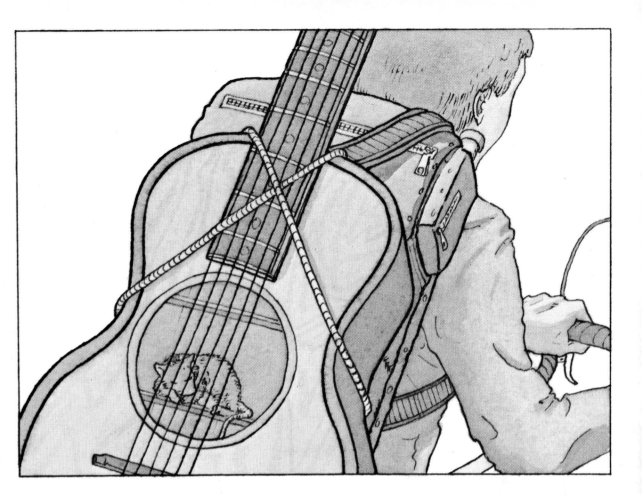

At last Pete came to the city. He asked
the first person he saw to tell him where he
could find the magic guitar. Then he went
right to the shop and bought the magic guitar.
Now Pete was very happy.

Pete set off for home with his magic guitar.
He traveled along, singing as he went.
Little did Pete know that inside the guitar
was Sylvester, sound asleep.

That night Pete stopped to rest
in a grassy meadow. It was very dark
and very quiet. Suddenly Pete heard music.
Pete sat up, and there was Sylvester
playing the guitar. "It is not a magic GUITAR!"
cried Pete. "It is a magic MOUSE. A mouse
with a musical ear!"

Sylvester stopped playing. He saw
the lovely grassy meadow. He heard
the lovely country sounds. He looked
at Pete, and Pete looked at him.

Sylvester went home with Pete. He played
the guitar while Pete sang. People came
from far away to listen to them. Pete and
Sylvester traveled here, and they
traveled there. They made soft music
and noisy music.

Sylvester traveled inside his fine house.
And sometimes at night he would sit
in his doorway, humming softly to himself.
Sometimes he was a city mouse, and sometimes
he was a country mouse. But at all times
he was a musical mouse — a mouse
with a musical ear!

Books to Enjoy

The Summer Maker

by Margery Bernstein and Janet Kobrin

The animals in this old Ojibway Indian story
go out looking for summer.

Big Boss! Little Boss! by Barbara Bottner

Two sisters learn something important
about each other.

Two Strikes, Four Eyes by Ned Delaney

Toby loves to play ball, but eyeglasses
can be a problem for a ball player.

Busybody Nora by Johanna Hurwitz

For Nora and her two hundred friends,
every day is an interesting day.

Odd Jobs by Tony Johnston

You'll laugh at the different kinds of work
that a boy named Odd Jobs finds to do.

Towers

MAGAZINE THREE

Contents

Send Wendell

by GENEVIEVE GRAY

Wendell lived with Mother, Father, William, Alice, and the baby, Anthony. Everybody was happy — most of the time. There was always work to do.

"William," Mother would say, "would you please put these newspapers outside?"

"I have to go play ball," William would say. "Send Wendell."

Or Father might ask Alice to go to the store.

"I have to do my homework," Alice would answer. "Send Wendell."

Wendell loved his mother and father very much. He liked to help them. But sometimes he wished — just a little — that William and Alice liked to help as much as he did.

One day Mother said, "Alice, go downstairs and see if there is any mail."

"I have to change my clothes," said Alice. "Send Wendell."

So Wendell went downstairs to get the mail.

Wendell found a letter in the mailbox.

It was for Mother and Father.

Mother read the letter and smiled.

"Uncle Robert is coming to see us!" she said. "He'll be here in a few days. All the way from California!"

Wendell knew about Uncle Robert. He had a farm in California. But California was far away. Wendell had never seen Uncle Robert.

The days went by, and the family got ready for Uncle Robert's visit. But Wendell did more to get ready than anyone else, except Mother and Father.

"Alice," said Mother, "take the baby for a walk while we clean the house."

"I have to finish making this dress," said Alice. "Send Wendell."

"William, go and pick up my good suit," said Father. "It's down the street at the cleaner's."

"I just got home from school," said William. "Send Wendell."

Mother gave Wendell the money to pay
the cleaner. Wendell went downstairs.

There by the front door was the tallest man
Wendell had ever seen. He was reading
the names on all the mailboxes.

Wendell stopped to stare at the man.
And the man turned and stared at Wendell.

Then the tall man began to laugh.

"You must be William," he said.

"No, I'm Wendell."

"I'm your Uncle Robert," said the tall man.

Wendell smiled.

"I'm going to the cleaner's," he said.
"I have to pick up my father's suit."

"You're a good boy to help out like that,"
said Uncle Robert. "I'll walk to the cleaner's
with you."

As they walked down the street, Uncle Robert
asked, "You never saw your grandfather,
d you?"

"No," said Wendell.

"When you grow up, you're going to look
just like him," said Uncle Robert.

Wendell smiled.

On the way back from the cleaner's,
Uncle Robert asked about the family.
Wendell told him a little bit about everybody.
But most of the time he just smiled happily.

When they got home, everyone talked at once.
William and Alice jumped up and down
and the baby gurgled.

That night dinner was special. Everybody ate
and listened hard to what Uncle Robert
was saying.

Father took the next day off from work,
and they all went to the zoo. On Sunday,
they had a picnic in the park.

In between times, Uncle Robert told Mother
and Father about his farm in California.
His own children were growing up, he said.
They all wanted to go to work in the city.
Before long, Uncle Robert would need someone
to help him on the farm.

All too soon it was time for Uncle Robert
to go back to California.

"Wendell," Uncle Robert said, "your mother
and father say that when you grow up
a little more, you can come to visit me
on the farm. Would you like to come
to California?"

"Yes," said Wendell. And he held tight
to Uncle Robert's hand.

The morning after Uncle Robert left,
Mother was getting the apartment straight again.

"Alice," said Mother, "Mrs. Wilson let us
have this big pan to use while Uncle Robert
was here. Take it back to her, please."

"I have to call somebody now," said Alice.
"Send Wendell."

But Wendell smiled. "I have to write
a letter to Uncle Robert," he said.

So Alice had to go anyway.

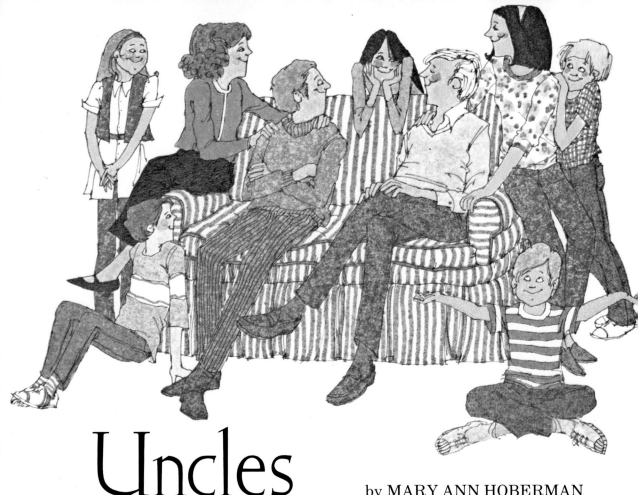

Uncles

by MARY ANN HOBERMAN

Uncles are brothers to fathers;

Uncles are brothers to mothers;

Uncles are fathers to cousins, of course,

And related to various others.

Uncles are husbands to aunts.

And I'm happy they happen to be;

But the very best thing about uncles, I think,

Is that uncles are uncles to me!

Pip Squeak
Mouse in Shining Armor

by ROBERT KRAUS

In all of Mousedom, there never lived
a braver mouse than Pip Squeak, Mouse
in Shining Armor.

Pip Squeak was the true enemy
of all dragonflies. On his green toad, Hopper,
he spent his days going after every dragonfly
he saw. But after a while, dragonflies were
too easy and Pip Squeak longed to fight
a real dragon.

To pick up pointers, Pip Squeak watched the seven knights who lived in the castle on the hill. "You're a mighty small knight with mighty big ears," said Sir Prise, who was the head knight.

"I'm not a knight," said Pip Squeak. "I am a mouse, and my ears are just the right size."

"Pardon me," said Sir Prise, "but I must hurry off and fight the Dreadful Dragon of Foe Fum Forest." So saying, he leaped upon his horse and rode off.

"Good luck," said Pip Squeak.

At sunset Sir Prise's horse returned
without Sir Prise. The other six knights were
quite upset. "Is there anything I can do
to help?" asked Pip Squeak.

"This is a job for a man, not a mouse,"
said Sir Pose. "And since I am a man, it is up
to me." So he leaped upon his horse and rode
off into Foe Fum Forest.

"Good luck, for what it is worth,"
said Pip Squeak.

Ten minutes later, Sir Pose's horse returned without Sir Pose. "That was fast," said Pip Squeak. The other five remaining knights, whose names were Sir Press, Sir Pass, Sir Port, Sir Plus, and Sir Pent, said nothing.

"Maybe it is a job for five men," said Pip Squeak.

"That's an idea," said Sir Pass, and the five knights leaped upon their horses and rode off into Foe Fum Forest to face the Dreadful Dragon.

Ten minutes later, five horses returned without their knights. "Five are as fast as one!" said Pip Squeak, quite surprised. Now all seven knights were gone, and there was only Pip Squeak left to fight the dragon. He was sorry for the knights, but happy for the chance.

So Pip Squeak rode bravely out into Foe Fum Forest. "I just hope I don't come back without *you*," said Hopper.

"No more than I," said Pip Squeak.

He had not gone far when he came upon
a witch. "You are a very small knight
with very large ears," said the witch.

"I am not a knight. I am a mouse," said
Pip Squeak, "and my ears are just the right size."

"Pardon me," said the witch. "Your shining
armor fooled me. You are not going to fight
the Dreadful Dragon of Foe Fum Forest, are you?"

"I am going to give it a try," said
Pip Squeak.

"I sell lucky charms to knights on their way to fight dragons," said the witch. "But in your case, I'm afraid I can promise nothing."

"That is quite all right," said Pip Squeak. "I don't need any luck, for I have a brave heart. But thank you anyway."

"Everybody could use a little luck," said Hopper, as he pushed on. The path was well-marked by signs which had been put there by the dragon himself. The dragon was afraid of no one and liked having visitors.

ALL VISITORS WELCOME

THIS WAY TO DRAGON

DRAGON THIS WAY

"You are a mighty small knight with mighty large ears," said an owl up in a tree. The owl had seen many knights travel by and not return.

"I am not a knight," said Pip Squeak. "I am a mouse and my ears are just the right size."

"Knight or mouse, you are not going to fight the Dreadful Dragon of Foe Fum Forest, are you?" asked the owl.

"I sure am," said Pip Squeak.

"Do you think it is wise?" asked the owl.

"I don't know if it is wise," answered
Pip Squeak, "but it is surely brave."

"What makes you think you can succeed when
everyone else has failed?" asked the owl.

"Every dragon has his weakness," said
Pip Squeak. "I have but to find it. *That* is
how I will succeed where so many have failed."

"That mouse not only has big ears, but he
also has a head on his shoulders," said the owl
as Pip Squeak and Hopper moved on.

The Dreadful Dragon!

Suddenly Pip Squeak and Hopper were face to face with the Dreadful Dragon! He was indeed dreadful, and for a second Pip Squeak almost lost his courage. But only for a second.

"My, my!" said the dragon. "You are a mighty small knight with mighty big ears."

"I am not a knight," said Pip Squeak. "I am a mouse and my ears are just the right size."

"A MOUSE!" cried the dragon. "The only thing in the world I dread!" — and he raced away in terror.

"Well," said Pip Squeak, "this was really a job for a mouse after all."

"Hooray! Hooray!" shouted Hopper.

"Hooray! Hooray!" rang seven voices in the distance.

"Did I hear an echo, or are those the seven knights whose horses returned without them?" asked Pip Squeak.

Pip Squeak followed his ears and there indeed, tied to a tree, were the seven knights whose horses had returned without them. Pip Squeak leaped from his toad and untied the knights, who began to sing, "For he's a jolly good mouse."

Then Pip Squeak led the freed knights,
singing and shouting, back to the castle
on the hill. "I am sure your horses will be
as glad to see you as I am," said Pip Squeak.

For his boundless courage, Pip Squeak was
made an Honorary Knight of the Kitchen Table.
"I dub thee Sir Pip Squeak," said Sir Prise.

Sir Pip Squeak's toad, Hopper,
was given a special place in the stable
alongside the horses of all the other knights.
"My dream has at last come true," said
Pip Squeak. "Although — now I am, indeed,
a small knight with rather large ears."

Making Music

What is music?

Music is different sounds
put together in a special order.

Sometimes the sounds are soft.
Sometimes the sounds are loud.

Sometimes the sounds are fast.
Sometimes the sounds are slow.

Sometimes the sounds are high.
And sometimes the sounds are low.

Many kinds of instruments
make those sounds.

The pages that follow tell about
some of these instruments.

This girl is playing a violin.
A violin has four strings.
It is played by drawing a bow
across the strings.

Here is another
instrument that has strings.

This boy is playing a clarinet.
Both the fingers and the mouth
are used to play this instrument.
The player must blow into one end
while using his fingers to open and
close the holes. The player's fingers
are kept busy because they must
work the keys, too.

This instrument is played
like the clarinet.

This is a trombone.

The word trombone means "big trumpet."

The trombone is played by blowing into one end while moving the long slide in and out.

Here is another instrument like the trombone.

Drums help to keep the beat
when many instruments
are played together.

Drums come
in many sizes.

This is a piano.

The piano has many keys. As each key
is pushed down, a different sound is heard.

Most instruments can be played alone,
or they can be played with other instruments.
When many people play different kinds
of instruments together, they are sometimes
called an orchestra. An orchestra must have
a leader. Some leaders use a baton
to help everyone play at the right time.

Fidelia

by RUTH ADAMS

Fidelia Ortega belonged to a musical family.

Fidelia's father, Papa Julio, played
the trumpet with a small band. The band
played for parties and dances. And it played
at the Mexican-American picnic each year.

Fidelia's big brother Alberto played
the trombone. Her sister Carmela
played the clarinet. Alberto and Carmela
were in the school orchestra. Once a year
the best players were asked to play
in the All City Orchestra.

Fidelia didn't play anything.

"You will have to wait," said Papa Julio.
"I don't have the money to buy
another instrument right now."

"You are too little," said Alberto.
"Your arms are too short to work
a trombone slide."

"You are too young," said Carmela. "You
need all your front teeth to play the clarinet."

Fidelia did not care about any of that.
She didn't want to play the trombone
or the clarinet. She wanted to play
a shiny brown violin.

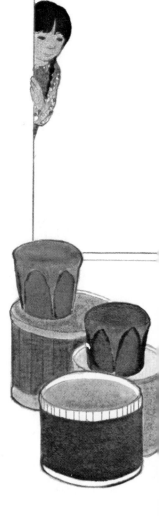

"But you can't," said Alberto. "Your arms
are too short. And your hands are too small.
You could not draw the bow across the strings.
You could not hold the strings down tight."

"You are just too young," said Carmela.
"Miss Toomey only lets older children
play the violin."

Fidelia thought, "I will talk
to Miss Toomey." So one morning Fidelia
stopped by the music room and looked in.
The orchestra was practicing. Up and down
went Miss Toomey's baton.

Fidelia could hear Alberto's trombone.
She could hear Carmela's clarinet.
And over them all she could hear the violins.

Fidelia tiptoed through the door so she
could listen more closely. "How lovely!"
she thought.

Fidelia closed her eyes and took another
step. *Crash! Bam! Bong!* She bumped
right into a set of drums.

Miss Toomey put down her baton. Everybody
stopped playing and looked at Fidelia.

"Oh, no!" whispered Carmela.

"Oh, no!" cried Alberto.

"What have we here?" asked Miss Toomey.

"It's our sister Fidelia," said Carmela.

"She wants to play in the orchestra,"
explained Alberto.

"Are you hurt, Fidelia?" asked Miss Toomey.
Fidelia shook her head.

"Come here and let me take a look at you,"
said Miss Toomey in a kind voice. Fidelia
walked slowly over to Miss Toomey.
Miss Toomey leaned down to talk to her.
"So you want to play in the orchestra?"

"Yes," whispered Fidelia.

"What instrument do you want to play?"
asked Miss Toomey.

"The violin," Fidelia whispered.

"You are a bit young to play the violin,"
said Miss Toomey. "But we *do* need
a tom-tom player for the Indian Dance.
Would you like to try?"

Fidelia looked up. "Yes, I would," she said.

So Fidelia played the tom-tom with
the orchestra. It was fun, but it wasn't
the same as playing a tune on a violin.

Every Monday Fidelia asked Miss Toomey
if she was big enough yet to play a violin.
Every Monday Miss Toomey shook her head
and said, "No, not yet, Fidelia."

Then one morning at orchestra practice,
Miss Toomey said, "Mrs. Reed is coming
next week. She will choose the players
for the All City Orchestra."

Everybody began to talk at once.

Tap! Tap! Tap! Miss Toomey's baton
called for order.

The orchestra began to practice
the Indian Dance. Fidelia beat her tom-tom,
but she wasn't happy. What could she play
for Mrs. Reed? If only she had a violin.

Then Fidelia had an idea.

Fidelia's Idea

On her way home from school, Fidelia stopped
at the store. "Do you have a small wooden box,
with a lid?" she asked the woman.

"Well, let's see," the woman answered.
"Here we are. I thought there was one
around somewhere."

"Oh, thank you," said Fidelia. She hugged
the small wooden box and hurried home.

Near Fidelia's house, workers were putting
up a new building. Fidelia went to the lot
and found a board that looked about right.

"Please, may I have this board?" she asked
one of the workers.

"Take all of them if you want them,"
the worker answered.

"I just want this one board, thank you,"
said Fidelia.

When Fidelia got home, she took the box
and the board into the garage.

Fidelia got the hammer. Then she emptied
a can of nails out on the workbench.
She picked out all the little thin nails.
Now she was ready to begin.

Tap! Tap! Fidelia's first nail went
through the lid of the box, but it missed
the thin side piece.

She placed the next nail with more care.

Tap, tap, tap. There. The box was nailed
shut. She placed her board across the box.

Tap-tap! Tap-tap! "Ouch!" Fidelia stuck
her thumb in her mouth. Then she
took it out and shook it.

Fidelia Gets Some Help

Just then Alberto came into the garage.

"What are you doing?" he asked.

"I'm making something," said Fidelia.
She stood in front of the workbench so Alberto
couldn't see what she was doing.

"Let me see. Come on. I won't laugh."
Alberto leaned over her shoulder.

Fidelia let him look. "The nails won't
go in straight," she said.

Alberto picked up the box and the board.
He looked them over. "What you need
is a brace," he said. "A brace will give
you something to hammer your nails into."

Alberto pulled a large box from
under the workbench. On one side of it was
written: ALBERTO ORTEGA. Across the lid
was written: KEEP OUT!

Alberto took out three small blocks of wood.
Then carefully he pulled up the lid
of Fidelia's small wooden box. He nailed
a block of wood against each end. He placed
the other block in the middle. A nail
through the bottom held it in place.

Tap! Tap! Tap! The lid was nailed
shut again.

"Now you have three braces to nail into,"
said Alberto.

"All right, you hold the board," said Fidelia.
"I'll hammer."

Alberto held the board tightly to the box.
Fidelia pounded a few good hard pounds.
The nails went in straight. Now the board
was on good and tight.

"That's great!" said Alberto. "What's next?"

"Strings," said Fidelia. "What can I use
for strings and pegs?"

"Well, you could use rubber bands
for the strings," said Alberto.

"That's a good idea," said Fidelia.
"Carmela saves rubber bands. For pegs,
I guess I'll just have to use nails."

Fidelia ran off to ask Carmela for some
rubber bands.

When Fidelia got back, Alberto was pushing his box back under the workbench. "Did you get the rubber bands?" he asked.

"Yes," Fidelia answered.

She picked up the hammer and nailed four nails at each end of the board. Then she pulled the rubber bands across the board and tied them around the nails.

Fidelia plucked the rubber bands with her fingers. *Twang, buzz, thwank.*

"It sounds terrible!" she cried.

Just then Carmela came in and looked
over Alberto's shoulder. "If you're trying
to make a violin," she said, "you need
a bridge for the strings to go over.

"Here, put this clothespin under
the rubber bands," she said. "Now try it."

Fidelia placed the violin carefully
under her chin. She plucked at the bands
with the fingers of her right hand. Then
she pressed down on the rubber-band strings
with her left hand.

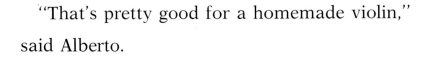

"That's pretty good for a homemade violin,"
said Alberto.

"It almost sounds like a tune," said Carmela.

"I wish I had a bow," said Fidelia.

"Make believe you have a bow," said Alberto.

After Carmela and Alberto left, Fidelia
practiced. By dinner time, she had practiced
so much that the ends of her fingers hurt.
But she knew just how to make the sounds
she wanted.

The Big Day

The day came for Mrs. Reed to choose
the players for the All City Orchestra. Fidelia
put her violin in a big bag and hurried off
to school.

The orchestra was tuning up when Fidelia got
to the door.

"Hurry up!" whispered Carmela. "We're going
to play the Indian Dance first. Mrs. Reed is
already here."

Fidelia put her bag down and got the tom-tom.
She played her very best.

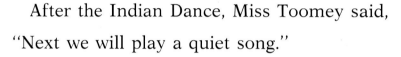

After the Indian Dance, Miss Toomey said,
"Next we will play a quiet song."

That was what Fidelia had been waiting for.
Carefully she took her violin out of the bag.
She put it under her chin. When she heard
the violins, she began to play.

Buzz . . . Buzz . . . Zubb . . . Zubb . . .!

Miss Toomey tapped her baton on her
music stand.

Buzz . . . Buzz . . . Suddenly Fidelia saw
that everyone else had stopped playing.
They were all looking at her.

"Oh, no!" whispered Carmela.

"Not *here*," cried Alberto.

Fidelia's face turned red.

"What do you have, Fidelia?" asked
Miss Toomey.

"It's a violin that I made," said Fidelia.

"May I see it?" asked Mrs. Reed. She looked
closely at the violin.

"You had a good idea," said Mrs. Reed.
"But I'm afraid you cannot play a real tune
on this violin."

"Oh, but I *can* play a real tune,"
cried Fidelia. "I've been practicing."

Then Fidelia put the violin under her chin and began to pluck at the rubber bands.

Sure enough, a good listener could hear a tune among the twanging, buzzing rubber-band noises.

Mrs. Reed was a good listener. She watched closely, too. "Where did you learn the right way to hold a violin?" she asked.

"And how did you know where to place your fingers on the strings?"

"I watched the others," said Fidelia. "And I did what Miss Toomey told them to do."

"Would you like to play a real violin?" Mrs. Reed asked.

"Oh, yes! But I am too little and not old enough yet," said Fidelia.

"Hm," said Mrs. Reed. "I think I have just the thing for you."

Then Mrs. Reed opened a small case. "This is a quarter-size violin, boys and girls. Let's see how it fits you, Fidelia."

It fit Fidelia just right.

"Fidelia," said Mrs. Reed, "the boy who was using this violin needs a bigger size now. So I am going to let you use this one. Miss Toomey will start you in the beginning string class. I will come back in a few weeks to see how you are getting along. How does that sound?"

"Wonderful!" cried Fidelia. "And can I play in the All City Orchestra?"

Mrs. Reed smiled. "Not this time," she said. "But I'm sure you'll do well enough to be in it in a year or so."

Fidelia tucked the little violin under
her chin. She set the bow on the strings.
"I'm ready, Miss Toomey."

Miss Toomey smiled. "Beginning string class
meets after lunch, Fidelia. Do you think
you can wait until then?"

246

That year Alberto and Carmela played
in the All City Orchestra. It was
Fidelia's turn to sit and listen. But she
didn't care. She had a violin just her size.
And she was in the beginning string class.

Everybody has to start somewhere.

Sound of Water

by MARY O'NEILL

The sound of water is:

Rain,

Lap,

Fold,

Slap,

Gurgle,

Splash,

Churn,

Crash,

Murmur,

Pour,

Ripple,

Roar,

Plunge,

Drip,

Spout,

Slip,

Sprinkle,

Flow,

Ice,

Snow.

248

Common Beginning Syllables

You have learned that a syllable is
a part of a word that can be said alone.
You also know that there are syllables
called common syllables that often come
at the ends of words. You will see
two of them in the sentences below.

1. Be **careful** when you cross the street.
2. There was a **lovely** butterfly on the tree.

There are other common syllables that
often come at the beginnings of words.

Look at the words in heavy black letters
in these sentences.

3. She planted small **round** bushes all
   around the yard.
4. He was standing on that **side** of the
   street **beside** the tree.

What was done to the first word in heavy
black letters in each sentence to make
the second word?

The letters a and be are often common syllables at the beginnings of words.

In many words that begin with the letters a or be, it will help you find out what those words are if you think the sounds those letters stand for in words like around and beside.

Use those sounds now to find out what the words in heavy black letters are in these sentences.

5. He took the car **apart.**
6. I have **become** tired of this game.
7. This coat **belongs** to Sharon.
8. Peter is reading the book **aloud.**

The letters a and be are often common syllables, but not always! In the word after, the letter a is not a common syllable. The first syllable in after is af.

In the word best, be is not a common syllable. The word best has only one syllable.

Two other syllables that often come
at the beginnings of words are <u>re</u> and <u>ex</u>.
Look at the words in heavy black letters in
these sentences.

9. I cannot **remember** my number.

10. I will be at home every day **except** Monday.

In many words that begin with <u>ex</u> or <u>re</u>,
it will help you to read those words if
you think of the sounds those letters stand
for in words like <u>remember</u> and <u>except</u>.

Use those sounds now to help you find out
what the words in heavy black letters are
in these sentences.

11. It was not hard to **repair** the car.

12. Tom **exchanged** trucks with his friend.

13. We had to **replace** the wood that we used.

When the letters re come at the beginning
of a word, they are very often a common
syllable and stand for the same sound
they stand for in remember, but not always!
In ready, the letters re are only a part of
the first syllable.

When the letters ex come at the beginning
of a word, they are always a common syllable
and have the same sound they stand for
in except.

When you meet new words that begin with
the letters a or be, it will often help
you to find out what those words are if you
think the sounds those letters stand for
in along and beside.

When you meet new words that begin with
the letters ex or re, it will often help you to
find out what those words are if you think
the sounds those letters stand for
in except and remember.

The Little Boy's Secret

by DAVID L. HARRISON

One day a little boy left school early
because he had a secret to tell his mother.
He was in a big hurry to get home so he
took a short cut through some woods where
three terrible giants lived. He hadn't gone far
before he met one of the giants standing
in the path.

When the giant saw the little boy, he looked down at him and roared, "What are you doing here? Don't you know whose woods these are?"

"I'm on my way home," answered the little boy. "I have a secret to tell my mother."

That made the giant quite angry. "Secret?" he bellowed. "What secret?"

"I can't tell you," said the little boy. "It wouldn't be a secret anymore."

"Then I'm taking you to our castle!" said the giant. Stooping down, he picked up the little boy and plopped him into his shirt pocket.

Before long, the first giant met the second giant. "What's that in your pocket?" he asked the first giant.

"A boy," he answered. "Says he has a secret he won't tell us."

When the second giant heard that, he chuckled. "Won't tell us, eh? Well, we'll just see about that! To the castle with him!"

The giants thumped on down the path.
In a short time they came to a huge castle
beside a muddy river.

At the door they met the third giant.
"What's in your pocket?" he asked
the first giant.

"A boy," he answered.

"A boy!" chuckled the third giant. He put
his huge eye close to the pocket and peered in.

"Says he has a secret he won't tell us,"
said the first giant.

When the third giant heard that, he laughed
a terrible laugh. "Won't tell us, eh?"
he asked. "Well, we'll just see about that!
On the table with him!"

The first giant took the little boy from
his pocket. He set him on the kitchen table.
Then all three giants gathered around
the table and peered down at him.

The little boy looked at the first giant.
He looked at the second giant. He looked at
the third giant. They were really enormous
and quite mean-looking.

"Well?" said the first giant.

"We're waiting," said the second giant.

"I'll count to three," said the third giant.
"One . . . two . . ."

The little boy sighed a big sigh.

"Oh, all right," said the little boy.
"I guess I can tell you. But if I do, you must
promise to let me go."

"We promise," answered the giants. But
they all winked at one another and crossed
their fingers behind their backs. They didn't
really mean to let him go at all.

The little boy turned to the first giant.
"Bend down," he said. When the giant leaned
down, the little boy whispered into his ear.

When the giant heard the secret, he leaped
up from the table. His knees shook. "Oh, no!"
he shouted. "That's terrible!" And he dashed
from the castle. He ran deep into the woods
and climbed to the top of a tall tree. He
didn't come down for three days.

The second giant scowled at the little boy.
"What's wrong with him?" he asked.

"Never mind," said the little boy. "Just
bend down." When the giant leaned down,
the little boy whispered into his ear.

When the giant heard the secret, he leaped
up so fast that his chair fell over. His eyes
rolled. "How awful!" he roared. And he raced
from the castle. He ran over a hill
and crawled into the deepest, darkest cave
he could find.

The third giant scowled a terrible scowl
at the little boy.

"What's wrong with them?" he asked.

"Never mind," said the little boy. "Just
bend down." When the giant leaned down,
the little boy whispered into his ear.

When that giant heard the secret, he jumped
up so fast that the table almost fell over.
His teeth chattered. "Help!" he cried.
"Help!" And he dashed from the castle
and dived headfirst into the muddy river.

The castle door had been left open.
Because the giants had promised the little boy
that he could go, he walked on home.

He told his mother his secret. *She* didn't
yell and run away. She put him to bed
and gave him some supper.

The next morning when the little boy
woke up, he was covered from head to toe
with bright red spots.

"Now I can tell everybody what my secret
was," he said with a smile. "My secret was . . .

I'M GETTING THE MEASLES!"

The Giant

by CHARLOTTE ZOLOTOW

I used to have a dream
long ago
about a giant
tall as a tree.

He came to the door
and said, "Come,"
holding his hand to me.

I never went
but now that I'm bigger
I wish I had.
He may have been a friendly giant
and I made him sad.

Just for Laughs

Gladys Told Me to Meet Her Here

by MARJORIE WEINMAN SHARMAT

My name is Irving. Gladys is my friend.
Gladys told me to meet her here. She's late.
Maybe she's not coming. Maybe she's lost.
When people are lost, it's terrible if no one looks
for them. I'm going to look for Gladys.

Gladys and I have big plans for today. We're going to play in the park all afternoon. Then she's coming to my house for supper — if I can find her.

Gladys and I have a secret place here where we leave messages for each other. I looked. Nothing.

GLA-A-A-A-A-DYS! GLA-A-A-A-A-DYS!

If she really is lost, she might get her picture in the paper. If she does, I'll tell everybody, "I know her."

Gladys is a really good and true friend. We found a new trail in the woods. Gladys named it The Irving Trail.

Poor Gladys. Where can she be? What if someone came up to me right now and asked, "Who is your best friend?"

I'd say, "Gladys." Just like that.

It's a good thing for Gladys that she has a friend like me. A friend who will walk

and walk

and walk

looking for her.

It's such a hot day! I could melt walking around. Or I could be lying on the ground with people standing over me. Then if Gladys came along, she'd be sorry.

Maybe Gladys won't show up until next winter. She'll find me stuck inside a big icicle. Then she'll really be sorry.

Gladys better have a good excuse. If Gladys is playing with Natalie, I'll never talk to her again. That will show her.

I am her good and true friend. I really am. I even tie her shoelaces for her when she has a sore thumb.

Gladys is going to be sorry. Next time I won't show up. Then she can wonder where *I* am. Gladys will look everyplace for me.

Say, maybe Gladys is looking for me right now. What if she thinks *I'm* lost? Maybe at this very minute she's telling the police that her good friend Irving is lost.

Yes. That's just what Gladys would do. She's my friend. I think I'll go back to where I was going to meet Gladys.

"Hello, Irving."

"Hello, Gladys."

That's Amy

by MARCI RIDLON

What makes Amy move so fast?
She never gets to places last.
She's always first to read the sign,
the first one up, the first in line,

That's Amy.

What makes Amy move so fast?
You're out in front, and she runs past.
You turn around, she's way ahead.
She's first all day, but last to bed,

That's Amy.

The Same But Not Quite the Same

A story writer can choose from many
words that have almost the same meaning.
But sometimes when the writer uses
one word instead of another, the meaning
is clearer to you.

Read these two sentences:

1. "You have a secret?" **asked** the giant.
2. "You have a secret?" **bellowed** the giant.

Now look at the words in heavy black
letters. Which word helped you to understand
better how the angry giant spoke?

Look at these two pictures.

Now read the two sentences below that tell
what the girl is saying. The words in heavy
black letters give the sentences a little
difference in meaning.

3. "I need some help!" she **called.**
4. "I need some help!" she **yelled.**

Which sentence seems to go better
with Picture B? Why does that sentence
seem better?

You will remember that in the story, *The String Collection*, Mr. Fergus had a big ball of string. If you were telling a friend about the size of this ball of string, which of these sentences might you say?

5. Mr. Fergus had a **large** ball of string.
6. Mr. Fergus had an **enormous** ball of string.

Since both words in heavy black letters mean about the same, you would be right no matter which sentence you said. But if you said it was *enormous,* your friend would probably have a better idea of how big it really was.

The two words in heavy black letters
in each pair of sentences below mean
about the same thing — but not quite!

Read the sentences. Then try to answer
the questions.

7. Father **raced** out to the car.

8. Father **ran** out to the car.

In both sentences Father went to the car
in a hurry. But in which sentence did
Father seem to go faster? Why?

9. Cindy said, "That was a **good** show."

10. Cindy said, "That was a **great** show."

In both sentences Cindy liked the show.
But in which sentence did she seem to
like it better? Why?

11. The rain **fell** against the window.

12. The rain **beat** against the window.

In both sentences it was raining.
But in which sentence did it seem
to rain harder? Why?

Ma Lien and the Magic Brush

by HISAKO KIMISHIMA

There once lived in China a poor peasant boy named Ma Lien. Day after day he worked hard in the fields so that he would have food to eat and a small hut to live in.

Ma Lien's great dream was to be an artist. But the boy did not even have one coin with which to buy a brush.

One day as he came from the fields,
Ma Lien saw the house of a well-known artist.
Going over to the high wall, Ma Lien looked in,
hoping to see the great man at work.

Not making a sound, he stood watching
the artist paint a picture of a mandarin.
At last the boy could be still no longer.

"Oh, great one," he said, "could you let me
have one of your brushes — an old one that
you don't need anymore? Then I, too, might
paint a picture."

On hearing this voice behind him, the artist
turned around. When he saw it was only
a poor peasant boy asking for one
of his brushes, he became very angry.

"So you think you would like to paint!"
he cried. "Away with you and back to your
fields!" And he ran the frightened Ma Lien
from his yard.

But Ma Lien did not let that stop him.
He drew pictures wherever he could. He used
a sharp stone to draw on a flat rock. Or he
used his fingers to draw in the wet sand
by the river.

When he came back to his hut at night,
he drew pictures on the wall. Before long,
he had covered the walls with pictures
of chickens, cows, sheep, and everything
he could think of.

One night as Ma Lien was lying on his bed,
he looked around his room at all the pictures
on the walls.

"Oh, if only I had a brush," he said.
"What beautiful pictures I would paint."
Suddenly there was a flash of light,
and standing before the boy was an old wizard.

"Ma Lien," he said. "You have worked
very hard, and now you shall have a brush.
Use it wisely, for it has great power."
And saying this, he handed the boy
a beautiful paintbrush.

Before Ma Lien could even say "thank you,"
the old man had disappeared.

Ma Lien hurried over to the one bare spot
on his wall. Quickly he painted a grand
and happy rooster. But he had no sooner
painted the last feather of the rooster's tail,
when the bird flew from the wall. The rooster
gave a great *cock-a-doodle-doo* and flew off
into the night.

"Now I know why the wizard said this brush
had great power," said Ma Lien. "Do not
worry, old wizard. I *will* use this brush wisely."

The next morning as Ma Lien was going
to the mountain to get wood, he went
by a rice field. There he saw a man
and a young boy pulling a heavy plow.

Ma Lien quickly went over to the wall
of an old hut and painted a strong
water buffalo. Again, just as he finished,
the buffalo jumped from the wall. It went
down to the rice field. With the help
of the buffalo, the man and the young boy
soon had the field ready for planting.

Just then the mandarin came by. He saw
the power of Ma Lien's magic brush.
He ordered his men to bring the boy
to the palace.

At the palace, the mandarin ordered the boy
to paint a pile of silver coins for him.
Ma Lien would not, for he remembered
the wizard's words. The mandarin had Ma Lien
put into prison with all his other prisoners.

Soon Ma Lien learned that the other prisoners
had done no wrong. The mandarin had them
put into prison so that he could take their lands.
"Don't worry," said the boy. "I will have
us all out of here before too long."

That night Ma Lien waited until the guards
had fallen asleep. Then quickly he painted
a door on the wall. The prisoners pushed
against it. The door flew open, and they all
ran out into the night.

The guards came running after Ma Lien,
but the boy easily got away on the fine horse
he had painted for himself.

The Mountain of Gold

Ma Lien knew he would not be safe
if he stayed on the mandarin's lands. So he rode
for many miles until he came to a strange village.

Here he helped anyone he could with
his magic brush. He painted buffaloes to help
the farmers in their fields. He painted toys
to keep the children happy.

One day Ma Lien saw some farmers
carrying water to their dried-up
fields. "That work is much
too hard for you," said Ma Lien.
And he set about painting
a fine water wheel. Now it would
be easier for the farmers
to bring water from the river
into their fields.

So it was that Ma Lien and
his wonderful brush came to be known
throughout the land. It wasn't long
before the mandarin learned where Ma Lien
was living. He sent his guards to the village.
When they found the boy, they took him back
to the palace.

The mandarin took away the brush at once.
Then he ordered that the boy be put back
into prison. "Without this brush, I don't think
he will get away so easily," the mandarin said.

Then the mandarin sent for the palace artist.
He ordered the artist to paint a picture
with the brush.

"What would you have me paint?"
asked the artist.

"A tree," said the mandarin. "A tree
with leaves of gold that will fall like rain
when I shake the branches."

The artist went right to work and soon had
a fine tree painted on the wall of the palace.

But when the mandarin hurried over
to shake the tree, he got no more than a bump
on the head. The tree was nothing but
a painting on the wall.

Now the mandarin could see that only
Ma Lien could paint pictures that would
become real. The mandarin sent for the boy.

"Ma Lien," he said softly, "if you will paint
a mountain of gold for me, I will let you go."

The boy saw a way to trick
the greedy mandarin. So he said that
he would do as he was asked.

The greedy mandarin's eyes lighted up.
He handed the brush to Ma Lien. "Paint me a
mountain of gold," he ordered.

The boy went to work at once. He painted
a big blue sea all across the wall.

"Why do you paint the sea?" shouted
the mandarin. "I ordered a mountain of gold."

"I have not finished," said the boy quietly.
And with that, he painted a great gold
mountain coming up out of the sea.

"Beautiful, beautiful!" cried the mandarin.
"Now paint me a ship. Then I can sail
to my mountain and bring back the gold."

In just a few seconds, Ma Lien had painted
a fine ship. The mandarin hurried on board
with his finest guards. Up went the sail.
And slowly the ship sailed out to sea.

"Too slow, too slow!" shouted the mandarin.
"Give us a wind to push us along."

Doing as he was ordered, Ma Lien painted
a wind storm. The wind came roaring down
and the sails filled out. The wind raced
across the water and made great waves
around the ship.

"Too much!" cried the mandarin angrily.
"You will sink my ship." But Ma Lien
went right on painting. The wind roared.
Huge waves crashed against the ship. Then
with a great *crrack*, the ship came apart
and disappeared in the stormy waters.

Once more Ma Lien went back to his life
with the peasants. He was always ready
to help them with their work. And never again
did anyone ask him to use his magic brush
for their own greedy wishes.

Books to Enjoy

The Magic Pot by Patricia Coombs

A poor man and his wife are helped by a magic pot that comes alive.

Evan's Corner by Elizabeth Starr Hill

Evan turns a small corner into a very special place.

The Beetle Bush by Beverly Keller

Everything Arabelle tries goes wrong, until she starts a garden.

Granny's Fish Story by Phyllis LaFarge

When Julie visits her grandmother, she learns about real and make-believe animals.

Hill of Fire by Thomas P. Lewis

This is a true story of what happened when a hill in Mexico began to burn.

Detective Mole by Robert Quackenbush

Here are five funny stories about Detective Mole.

Consonants

ch	chair	**th**	think	**sh**	shell
wr	wrong	**kn**	know		

br	branch	**bl**	block	**sc**	scare
cr	creak	**cl**	clown	**sm**	small
dr	dragon	**fl**	flower	**sn**	sneeze
fr	friend	**gl**	glass	**sp**	space
gr	grass	**pl**	please	**st**	story
pr	pretty	**sl**	sleep	**sw**	swim
tr	tractor				

qu	quack
squ	squirrel

thr	three	**spr**	spring
	throw	**str**	strong

Sounds for **c**	cat	pencil
Sounds for **g**	game	cage

Turn the page.

Vowels

Short Vowel Sounds

a   hat crack

e   leg get

i   swim six

o   frog rock

u   sun truck

Long Vowel Sounds

a   brave made

e   free green

i   kite slide

o   home stone

u   mule use

Two vowels together often stand for just one sound.

ai   paint   **ee**   feet

ay   play   **oa**   boat

Two vowels together can stand for different sounds in different words.

oo   school   **ea**   beach

     book   bread

More Vowel Sounds

_____ **y**   fly   _____ **y**   baby

ow   owl   **ew**   few   **aw**   saw
bowl

ar park   **or** short
er her   **ur** turn
ir bird

are share   **ire** tire   **ore** store   **ure** sure

ere   here   there   were

When you come to a new word —

Read to the end of the sentence.

Think about what the sentence is saying.

Think about the sounds letters stand for.

Does the word you named make sense in the sentence?

Does the word you named have the right sounds?

"The Great Eraser," from *Gingerbread Children*, by Ilo Orleans. Follett and Company. 1973. Reprinted by permission of Friede Orleans Joffe.

"I Like to Swing," by Regina Sauro. Reprinted from *Instructor*. Copyright © June 1958 by Instructor Publications, Inc. Used by permission.

"Josefina February," from *Josefina February*, by Evaline Ness. Copyright © 1963 by Evaline Ness. Reprinted by permission of Charles Scribner's Sons.

"Just for Laughs," adapted from *Jokes and Puns*, by Irving Wasserman; James Moffett, Senior Editor; *Interaction* Language Arts Program. Copyright © 1973. Used by permission of Houghton Mifflin Company.

"Lions in the Grass," from *Lions in the Grass: The Story of the Dandelion, a Green Plant*, by Phyllis S. Busch. Text copyright © 1968 by Phyllis S. Busch. Reprinted by permission of Curtis Brown, Ltd.

"The Little Boy's Secret," adapted with permission from *The Book of Giant Stories* by David L. Harrison, 1972. Illustrations © 1972 by Philippe Fix. Published by McGraw-Hill Book Co. and Jonathan Cape Limited.

"A little yellow cricket," from *Singing for Power: The Song Magic of the Papago Indians of Southern Arizona*, by Ruth Murry Underhill. Originally published by the University of California Press; reprinted by permission of the Regents of the University of California.

"Ma Lien and the Magic Brush," adapted from *Ma Lien and the Magic Brush*, by Hisako Kimishima. Illustrated by Kei Wakana. Text copyright © 1968 by Parents' Magazine Press. Used by permission of Parents' Magazine Press.

"A Mouthful of Words," ("Of all the felt. . . .") excerpt from *Ready or Not, Here I Come* by Carl Withers. Copyright © 1964 by Carl Withers. Used by permission of Grosset & Dunlap, Inc.

"My Kite," by Myra Cohn Livingston. From *The Moon and a Star*, © 1965 by Myra Cohn Livingston. Reprinted by permission of Harcourt Brace Jovanovich, Inc.

"The Night the Lights Went Out," adaptation of pp. 47–54 from *Nora and Mrs. Mind-Your-Own Business*, by Johanna Hurwitz. Text copyright © 1977 by Johanna Hurwitz. Used by permission of William Morrow & Company.

"Pip Squeak, Mouse in Shining Armor," adapted text of *Pip Squeak, Mouse in Shining Armor*, by Robert Kraus. Text copyright © 1971 by Robert Kraus. A Windmill Book. Used by permission of Thomas Y. Crowell, Publishers.

"Send Wendell," from *Send Wendell*, by Genevieve Gray. Copyright © 1974 by Genevieve Gray. Used by permission of the author and McGraw-Hill Book Company.

"Six Special Places," adapted from *Six Special Places*, by Monica De Bruyn. Text © 1975 by Monica De Bruyn. Used by permission of Albert Whitman & Company.

"Sound of Water," from *What Is That Sound!*, by Mary O'Neill. Text copyright © 1966 by Mary O'Neill. Reprinted by permission of Atheneum Publishers.

"The String Collection," by Mary Radloff. Copyright © 1977 by *Highlights for Children, Inc.*, Columbus, Ohio. Used by permission of the publisher.

"Sylvester, the Mouse With the Musical Ear," adapted from *Sylvester, the Mouse with the Musical Ear*, by Adelaide Holl. Copyright © 1973, 1961 by Western Publishing Company, Inc. Used by permission of the publisher.

"That's Amy," by Marci Ridlon. Copyright © 1976 by Marci Ridlon. Used by permission of the author.

"Uncles," from *Nuts to You and Nuts to Me*, by Mary Ann Hoberman. Copyright © 1974 by Mary Ann Hoberman. Reprinted by permission of Alfred A. Knopf, Inc. and Russell & Volkening Inc.

Credits

Illustrators: pp. 7–26, Ronald Himler; pp. 27–30, 58–61, 100–102, 136–139, 249–252, 276–279, Bob Barner; pp. 31–38, Claudette Boulanger; pp. 40–55, Freya Tanz; pp. 56–57, Sue Thompson; pp. 62–63, Carol Nicklaus; pp. 69–83, Ellen Appleby; p. 84, Bari Weissman; pp. 89–97, Rosekrans Hoffman; pp. 98–99, Ruth Brunner-Strosser; pp. 103–120, Jurg Furrer; p. 135, Mila Lazarevich; pp. 140–155, True Kelley; pp. 156–157, Robert Masheris; pp. 158–165, Carol Way Leeson; p. 166, Dorothea Sierra; pp. 167–186, David Wiesner; pp. 191–201, Jane Dyer; p. 202, Blanche Sims; pp. 203–216, Doug Cushman; pp. 223–247, Deborah Ray; p. 248, Susan Russo; pp. 253–263, Philippe Fix; p. 264, Lane Yerkes; p. 265, Arlene Dubanevich; pp. 266–274, Diane Paterson; p. 275, Rosalynn Schanzer; pp. 280–298, Kei Wakana.

Photographers: p. 39, Michael Malyszko; pp. 64–68, Deidra Stead; pp. 121–134, John Running; pp. 217–222, Lou Jones.

Book cover, title page, and magazine covers by Andrzej Dudzinski